COMMUNICATION SERIES

How to Coach an Effective Team

Leadership That Gets Results

Written by
Micki Holliday and Joe Gilliam

NATIONAL PRESS PUBLICATIONS
A Division of Rockhurst University Continuing Education Center, Inc.
6901 West 63rd Street • P.O. Box 2949 • Shawnee Mission, Kansas 66201-1349
1-800-258-7246 • 1-913-432-7757

National Press Publications endorses nonsexist language. In an effort to make this handbook clear, consistent and easy to read, we have used "he" throughout the odd-numbered chapters, and "she" throughout the even-numbered chapters. The copy is not intended to be sexist.

How to Coach an Effective Team —
Leadership That Gets Results

Published by National Press Publications, Inc.
Copyright 2000 by National Press Publications, Inc.
A Division of Rockhurst University Continuing Education Center, Inc.

All rights reserved. No part of this publication may be reproduced or utilized in any form by any means, electronic or mechanical, including photocopying, recording or by any information storage and retrieval systems, without permission in writing from National Press Publications.

Printed in the United States of America

7 8 9 10

ISBN 1-55852-249-2

Table of Contents

Introduction iii

Acknowledgments v

1 The Effective Team 1
    What Is an Effective Team? 1
    What Does It Take? 3
    When Does Coaching Come Into Play? 3
    Performance Misconceptions and Barriers 4
    What Is Needed to Lead an Effective Team? 5
    How Are Coaching and Leading Related? 8
    Coaching a Team: the Skills Required 9
    Summary 11

2 The Team Leader 13
    Responsibilities of an Effective Leader 14
    Issue of Motivation 16
    Insights a Leader Must Possess 20
    Rethink Your Views of a Team 22
    Values, Characteristics of an Effective Leader 22
    Summary 25

3 A Coaching Model 29
    What Is the Model? 30
    The Five-Step Staff Coaching Model 32
    Leadership Behaviors in the Model 33
    To Develop, Support and Grow a Team 34
    When to Cheer 37
    What It Means to Lead 38
    Why People Don't Do What They Are Supposed to Do 39
    Summary 40

4 "Coaching" the Team 43
    The Coach's Role With a Team 43
    What Does It Mean to Coach a Team? 44
    Clarify the Role of Coach 45
    The Coach Is a Hands-On Leader 46
    The Team in Which the Leader Sees Some Potential 47
    Why Is the Role of Coach Beneficial? 48

  Goal — New Levels of Performance 48
  Why Some Leaders Don't Coach 48
  Pitfalls 50
  Communicating as a Coach 52
  Characteristics of a High-Performance Coach 54
  Summary 55

5 "Mentoring" the Team **57**
  What Does Mentoring Mean? 58
  The Benefits of Mentoring 58
  Why Leaders Should Mentor 60
  Why Don't Leaders Mentor More? 60
  When Mentoring Is Most Beneficial 61
  Actions and Techniques of the Mentor 63
  Smart Questions 64
  Summary 66

6 "Counseling" the Team **69**
  What Is a Counselor? 69
  When to Counsel 70
  The Benefits of a Counselor Role 70
  Why Leaders Don't Counsel 71
  Confrontation 72
  How to Use the Counseling Role Effectively 74
  Actions of a "Counselor" 75
  A Word of Caution 77
  Checking Out Your Counseling Skills 78
  Summary 80

7 Developing Habits for High Performance **83**
  Personal Growth 84
  Moving In and Out of One's Comfort Zone 85
  High-Performance Skills 86
  Character of a High-Performance Coach 89
  Summary 89

  Appendix A **93**

  Appendix B **105**

  Index **107**

INTRODUCTION

In Tom Peters' book *In Search of Excellence*, the author makes this statement: "In the future, a manager will have to be a coach and a cheerleader." That concept requires a whole new paradigm, which means we must have a paradigm shift as leaders. We must have a whole new way of thinking. There's only one way to change the way we think and that's to take in new information. When you take in new information, you reprogram the computer (the mind), and you change the way you think. You not only change the way you think, but you change the way you feel and you change the way you behave. So we must have a paradigm shift. We have to begin to think not like a manager, but like a coach.

Before we change to this new paradigm — this new way of thinking — I want you to go back for just a moment and remember when you became a manager. You were a member of the team and you were a real superstar on that team. You got results. You carried the ball. You scored the touchdowns. You were the person who was always winning the accolades. So they called you into the office one day. "Have a seat," they said, and they closed the door. "Rise. Kneel." They took out a big sword and said, "Now we knight you a manager. Rise, go forth and manage." But of course, they gave you no new information. Without new information, you couldn't change the way you think. You didn't change the way you feel about yourself or other people, and you didn't change the way you behave. You did continue to get results. The only thing that changed was your position and your title. You still saw yourself in the same way, and continued to get results because you were comfortable doing so.

There's only one problem: The people on your team had a paradigm shift in the way they saw you. Now they saw you as the manager. You were the one who should lead them. But you continued to get results on your own, because you had to get results due to the new title and position. You came in at six o'clock in the morning, but the rest of the team didn't arrive until eight. There were times you were there until eight, nine or ten o'clock at night because you had to get results.

COACHING

Think about a football team. Suppose the game is over. The teams have left. You're sitting in the stands, and the two coaches are still running up and down the field trying to score points. They are still trying to win the game. What would you think of these two coaches? You'd think they were crazy. Of course, you get the message. A manager who continues to get results by himself is crazy.

What I want you to do when you read this book is take in new information. I want you to have a paradigm shift. I want you to change the way you feel, not only about yourself but also about your people. Now you still get paid to get results, no matter what your title is or how you see yourself. If the coach doesn't get results, they don't fire the team, they fire the coach.

The way to get results is through your people. Your people become your greatest asset. In 1978 Ferdinand Fournies wrote, in *Coaching for Improved Work Performance*, "A technician is a person who gets results. A manager or coach is a person who gets results through people." You need to see your people as your greatest asset. It is through your people that you will get results. That doesn't mean that you don't still get results, but you get more results through your people. Invert the pyramid of your organizational chart. Put your customers or clients first and then your people, your team members, next, because they are the way you will meet the customers' needs. As a manager you are underneath both your customers/clients and your team, so now your job is to support and develop people because they are the ones who will get the results.

This book will provide you with the information to *coach*, *mentor* and *counsel* your team members as they move from present performance to new levels of performance. This will make you the coach of a winning team.

Coach Joe

Throughout the book you will find *"Coach Joe Says,"* which are particular stories or statements that Coach Joe uses to illustrate a point or an idea. Use these to build your coaching skills with ease.

I want to thank my teams who, over the last 20 years, have allowed me to coach many people to success:

ACKNOWLEDGMENTS

My Family Team

Nancy, my wife of 36 years

Angie, Sean and Karis, my children

Dan, my son-in-law

Cole, Sarah, Olivia, Nathaniel and Seth, my grandchildren

My National Seminars Team

Especially Micki Holliday, who has coached me and worked with me so much over the last 10 years.

Coaching

1 THE EFFECTIVE TEAM

Have you ever been on a relay team? Remember what it was like when you had to trust other people to pass the baton, or give their very best, cheer each other on and use the strategies your team agreed on in order to win the race? That is a wonderful example of a team. Achieving the goal would not have been possible without the best efforts of every person on the team, including the team captain or team leader. Successful leaders know how to work with the team to help bring out the very best in each team member. They know how to coach team members for greater performance. Let's take a closer look at what it takes to build an effective team.

What Is an Effective Team?

An effective team is a group of people working toward a common purpose, with the actions and activities of the members interlinked to achieve the goal or purpose. An effective team requires the participation of every member in order to be successful. Teams require a clear goal, an informal system of communicating and participating, an informal climate and established decision-making procedures.

Effective leaders realize that all teams go through stages and know how to guide the team through each stage. When the team is in the structuring stage, the leader coaches the team in setting ground rules and defining the

COACHING

boundaries. The leader also encourages each team member to realize he is responsible for helping the team to achieve the best possible result. Empowerment and involvement are critical at this stage. This is the time to excite and inspire your team members.

The next stage the team goes through is the settling stage. At this point the team is focusing on its agenda; expectations are being stated and restated so the team can adjust and take full advantage of the strengths each team member brings to the table. Team members want to know what is expected of them and exactly how they fit into the overall plan. This is when it's important to mentor the team so members recognize the relationship of their team to other teams in the organization and to the organization as a whole.

The third stage is the problem-solving stage. As team members begin working together it's normal for them to experience conflict. During this phase you might see enthusiasm begin to wear down, and some confusion and anger from team members. The team defines rules for handling anger and resistance, and looks for ways to stay focused on the problem rather than on a person or another team that may not be performing the way they should. This is the time when the team needs to establish an acceptable approach to resolving conflict. The leader needs to be skilled in counseling teams and other groups of people in how to develop excellent problem-solving skills.

The learning stage is the stage where the team really starts to make progress and productivity begins. There is growth in the team, which is recognized and rewarded. Individual members of the team also grow personally and look for ways to continue that personal growth. One sign of a team in the learning stage may be the cross-training of team members, so that regardless of what's happening the team can still fulfill its goal or purpose. Training, and more training, is necessary for the success of any team.

Then teams move to the performing stage where they are able to go about their business with confidence. There's a high level of trust among the team members, and that encourages members to give their very best effort for the good of the team. The team has clear direction. Team members know the

THE EFFECTIVE TEAM

expectations, are aware of time frames, have a method for handling conflict, and are building skills for problem solving. This is the finest hour of any team — when it all comes together effectively and efficiently.

What Does It Take?

Glenn Parker, who wrote *Team Players and Teamwork*, outlines the following characteristics of an effective team. He says an effective individual or an effective team has a clear purpose and knows why the team exists and what it or the individual should be doing. There is also an informal climate that encourages everyone to participate and speak out even when their views are contrary to the majority. Effective teams are made up of individuals who practice good listening skills and know how to deal successfully with conflict. These teams know that differences need to be expressed so the team can reach consensus, and everyone agrees to support the outcome. This team builds open communication so each team member clearly knows his role and work assignments. This leads to shared leadership, which means everyone takes responsibility for meeting the task and processing needs of the team. The effective team also builds external relationships with people outside the team, so the team can communicate its successes to others, which increases its credibility. Also, successful teams know that diversity is a strength. They value the achievement of their objective, so they take time to evaluate by asking the question, "How can we improve our team or our organization?"

When Does Coaching Come Into Play?

The leader who desires to help the team to achieve its highest level of success must be prepared to coach, mentor or counsel the team and its members as the team moves toward the performance goal. Even though there is shared leadership on an effective team, someone is still responsible for seeing that the team stays focused on its task or goal and that everyone is moving toward accomplishing that task. The team may become nonproductive because of conflicts among its members. The leader must decide

COACHING

whether it is a conflict arising out of issues, personality conflicts, misunderstanding about a member's role on the team, or a lack of understanding of the expectations of each team member. The leader determines the underlying issue and then begins to coach team members to move beyond the problem. The leader is responsible for seeing that the problem is accurately diagnosed and leading members to solve the problem.

The leader is crucial in setting the tone of trust among individuals. To help achieve this, the leader may lead them to experience some team-building activities. It is difficult for the team to learn to trust without opportunities to build that trust. Team members need to function together enough to learn to depend on each other to get the job done. The leader who is functioning in the coaching role provides these kinds of experiences for the team. When the leader sees that the team is bogged down in non-essentials or non-issues, it's time to go into the coaching mode and begin moving the team to achieve its task.

Respect is another requirement for high performance. The leader must have respect for each team member, and the members must respect the leader as well as each other. This respect is reflected in the ground rules the team establishes when the team is structuring. It is also reflected in the way team meetings are conducted and team members respond to each other. Each person is given the opportunity to participate, share ideas and suggestions, and each idea or solution is given equal time. Team members are encouraged to use their strengths to help the team accomplish the tasks it has been given.

Performance Misconceptions and Barriers

One misconception or barrier to building an effective team is that all groups of people who have a common goal are a team. A common task is not the central requirement for a team — it's being interdependent on each other to accomplish the task. The leader has to be aware of the need to move the team from being a work group to being a real team. In a team, there is a great deal of support and encouragement from the various team members to get the task

THE EFFECTIVE TEAM

done, and team members are willing to jump in and help each other so the task is completed on time.

Abraham Lincoln had a favorite riddle: "If a dog has four legs and a tail and you call the tail a leg, how many legs does the dog have?" Of course, the answer is four! Calling a tail a leg doesn't make it a leg. In just the same way, calling the work group a team doesn't make it a team. Too many teams have failed because they were really just work groups, and the leader didn't coach them to become a team.

A barrier for teams to overcome is the independent spirit that many people have and are recruited for. We haven't necessarily been taught "one for all and all for one." Many have been raised to believe, "I need to look out for number one!" That attitude makes it difficult for us to be team players, because it means sharing ourselves with others and letting them have the advantage of our knowledge and skills as well as any information we might have. In an environment where we've been told that knowledge is power, this can be a threatening concept.

Another barrier is the spirit of competition that permeates many workplaces as well as our personal lives. Too much competition can slow or even stop communication. This can cause team members to withhold information and so sabotage the team effort. This compromises the effectiveness of the organization and builds a bad attitude among team members and among different teams in the same organization.

What Is Needed to Lead an Effective Team?

The team leader has to be willing to help the team move beyond these misconceptions and barriers. The team leader helps the team realize that its finest hour is when all are functioning together, sharing ideas and strengths, interdependent on each other to achieve a goal. This concept requires a great deal of skill on the part of the leader, but the good news is that the needed skills can be learned. The leader has to be willing to change, grow and move out of his own comfort zone. This will be good for him and the team, because

COACHING

he will be asking team members to move out of their comfort zones and grow, so he will set the pace and show by example. In other words, "he'll walk the walk, not just talk the talk."

— *Coach Joe Says ...*

When my children were growing up, I saw the necessity of walking my talk. I was the leader/coach, and they were my team. I read self-improvement books and listened to tapes in order to have the knowledge and information I needed to help them grow. I believe that is why Angie, Sean and Karis all have a desire to learn today. What an asset this desire to learn has been for them as they move into adulthood.

The team leader needs to be someone who is willing to invest himself in the lives of others. His behavior as the leader is critical to building trust and open communication. He must encourage discussion of problems and concerns while responding in a non-judgmental way. Being willing to model this type of behavior helps build trust among the team members. They see that he is willing to invest himself in them and their future. It's by this investing in others that the leader is able to help build trust in the team.

Trust is a critical factor for the team to function effectively. The leader sets the stage for this trust factor to build. Therefore, the leader must be someone who is constantly building people skills. This means the leader needs to be developing communication skills as well as listening skills. The leader not only improves his communication and listening skills, but also gives team members opportunities to build their people skills. This should be one of the primary goals of the team leader.

In addition to helping team members build people skills, the team leader needs to periodically involve the team in team-building activities. This will help members learn to work together more effectively because it is another tool to help them develop trust. Many team-building activities will also give members an opportunity to improve problem-solving skills, accomplishing two goals with one activity.

THE EFFECTIVE TEAM

The effective team leader motivates the team. The leader needs to be a cheerleader for team members as they move toward the goals, complete the task, deal effectively with conflict, and use their strengths for the benefit of the whole team. The leader helps team members remember that every member of the team is vital and necessary, and helps them develop their skills, especially their skills at being a team member.

The leader also provides recognition and appreciation to team members, which helps prevent burnout and encourages growth. Researcher J. C. Staehle discovered that American workers listed the number one cause of job dissatisfaction as failure of bosses to give recognition for what they had accomplished. When team members don't receive recognition for the job performed, they begin to feel unnecessary or that anyone could do their job. When team members start to feel this way, they begin to focus more on their own needs and less on how they benefit the team or the organization. Then the team becomes dysfunctional and unable to accomplish the goals or tasks it has been given.

— *Coach Joe Says ...*

Coach John Wooden always required his players to praise the teammate who had passed the ball when a basket was scored. A player once said, "What if he isn't looking when I come back up the court?" Wooden said, "He will always be looking."

To effectively lead people, the leader must also be willing to nurture individual members. Nurturing means the leader will spend time with individuals. He can help people plan their own personal accomplishment goals and an action plan to achieve these goals. These goals can be designed to help the team member build a technical skill or improve interpersonal skills. This requires the team leader to make an investment of time in the individual members of the team. The benefit is enormous, though, because not only does the team member benefit, but so does the entire team.

COACHING

— *Coach Joe Says ...*

Roger Enrico, CEO of Pepsi Cola, personally conducts 100 leadership seminars with his people each year.

The successful leader also encourages discussion and development of new ideas, new ways of doing things and new ways of looking at the same opportunities or circumstances. There is an open discussion of ideas, and creative solutions to challenges (there are no problems here!) are encouraged. Often team members are not used to functioning in this type of an open environment, so the team leader needs to establish an atmosphere of openness that encourages growth.

The most important thing the team leader can do is to continue the learning and growing process personally. The team will see him as someone who "walks the walk" and lives out what he is teaching them. This means he is continually building people skills, problem-solving skills, an ability to deal with change, and a willingness to think outside the box.

How Are Coaching and Leading Related?

A leader must have followers, which indicates a degree of responsibility for the people he is leading. This means he needs to be involved in coaching or building their skills. Webster's Dictionary defines "coach" as "to train intensively, to instruct, direct or prompt." The dictionary defines "lead" as "to guide on a way especially by going in advance, to direct on a course or in a direction." In order to lead, he will be expected to coach his team, because there will be times when members won't have the skills needed to handle the situation.

An example of this type of leadership would be in conflict resolution, or "civilized disagreement" as it has been called. The team may need some coaching in the skills needed to resolve conflicts, which will allow the team to continue working together successfully. This means the team leader will help members as they are setting their ground rules during the structuring stage, so

THE EFFECTIVE TEAM

they have boundaries for interpersonal relationships. When conflict occurs, he will guide the team through the conflict and help members grow personally and professionally at the same time. The leader has many different roles to fill, so he needs to be constantly building his own people skills in order to be an effective leader for his team.

Coaching a Team: the Skills Required

Technical skills are required if the leader is to inspire confidence in team members. "If you don't know how to do the job, how can you expect to lead others to successfully complete the job?" is the question team members ask. As you move up in the organization, however, technical skills become less important and interpersonal skills more important. The team leader's ability to be a visionary and see the big picture becomes critical at the highest level in organizations. At all levels the leader is expected to be able to motivate, inspire, organize and train his team to function at its maximum achievement level. Let's take a closer look at some of these skills required for coaching a team.

Leaders have the ability to motivate their employees. We won't go into the debate about whether a team leader can actually motivate employees or just provides the atmosphere of support and encouragement so that employees can motivate themselves to get the task done. Regardless of where the leader stands in this discussion, there is no doubt that team members need to be motivated and that coaching can positively affect morale.

Leaders value their team members. They realize that each member is unique and has strengths that contribute to the overall success of the team. The team leader then helps the members to strengthen those skills and rely on the strengths of others to compensate for their weaknesses. When the leader invests his time in valuing team members, the benefit is enormous. The member is encouraged and inspired to continue developing and growing. The team and the organization are strengthened. Even the leader can benefit because it's exciting and fulfilling to see team members develop and grow.

COACHING

Leaders create a vision for their team members. Leaders have the ability to stretch team members to accomplish the goal or task. Leaders also know that if the goal is unreasonable or unattainable, it becomes a discouragement to the team rather than a motivator. The leader is capable of leading the team in breaking down a big vision into smaller visions or goals that the team feels are attainable. The skilled leader knows there is a thin line between goals and visions that stretch and ones that defeat.

Leaders inspire team members to action by directing their creativity and energy toward accomplishing the goals and tasks of the team. Effective team leaders also encourage the team to look at the processes being used to accomplish the goal. Is there a better way? Is there a faster way to accomplish this task? Is this the best use of our time and resources? These are all questions team leaders keep before the team. This accomplishes several things:

1. Helps team members deal more easily with change if they are used to questioning what's being done and how it's being done.

2. Encourages creativity among the team members if they're always looking for new and different ways of accomplishing their tasks.

3. Utilizes the strengths and minimizes the weaknesses of various team members.

4. Helps develop leadership skills of team members. This is encouraging to them because they see personal growth as a result of being part of this team!

As Tom Peters noted in his book *In Search of Excellence*, the team leader needs to be the head cheerleader for the team. He leads them to believe in themselves, to develop their skills and abilities, to strive for a higher level of personal and professional achievement and, in turn, pass on what they've learned to someone else. It becomes an ongoing process that benefits the people in the organization and also benefits the organization. People need to be encouraged to greater heights of achievement. They need to know that someone believes in their ability to achieve. Team members need to know that the leader is not only willing to help them achieve higher levels of growth, but he expects them to continue to learn and grow.

The Effective Team

Summary

An effective team leader must know what makes an effective team. That means realizing that all teams go through five stages and that there's a need to keep the team focused and functioning. The effective team leader also knows the characteristics of effective teams and works to help his team become more effective. He develops his own technical skills as well as people skills so he can build an effective team. He helps the team in the team-building process and realizes that his primary task is to develop people, not just get the job done. The team leader stretches and grows the members of his team so they all achieve more because they are working together as an effective team. This is done though coaching, mentoring and counseling.

It's been said that all glory comes from daring to begin. Dare to begin building an effective team and see the glory that comes — the glory that comes to the leader and also to the people he builds, strengthens, encourages and empowers as team members. What greater glory could any leader want?

REFLECTIONS

Think of the best team leader you've ever had.

What are some of the reasons you think this person is the best leader you've ever had? List the behaviors he or she exhibited:

Of all the behaviors you listed, which one do you think is the most important and why?

What ONE behavior will you commit to develop so you can be a more effective leader?

Reflections

2 THE TEAM LEADER

The excitement of being a leader is being able to influence the lives of other people. A leader is able to help them grow, expand, explore new capabilities and strengths they weren't even aware they possessed. She is in the business of building people, and there isn't a task more challenging or exciting. Let's take a closer look at some of the things she is responsible for as an effective leader. Her success as a leader depends on her ability to work effectively through people.

In this chapter, the behavior of an effective team leader will be examined, in order to help build leadership skills. The rest of the book will be devoted to helping build three essential leadership skills — coaching, mentoring and counseling.

The leader will need to function as a coach when job skills need to be improved. When she needs to help the team member with personal and professional development beyond what is needed for the task or function of the present team, she moves into the mentor role. When she works with people, some of them will have problems that interfere with the job, which then requires her skills as a counselor. This does not mean she will provide professional counseling for the person, but simply help them stay focused on job responsibilities while dealing with things in their personal or professional lives that may be very traumatic. Some examples might be a relationship that is falling apart, the death of a parent, or the severe illness of a child. It could also be doubts about one's career or the conflict between work and personal time. These traumatic experiences are part of the reality of life, and she needs

COACHING

to be prepared to help team members deal with them effectively. An effective leader has certain basic competencies regardless of which role she is functioning in, so let's take a closer look at some of them.

Responsibilities of an Effective Leader

As we saw in the last chapter, an effective leader is someone who is able to guide the team as it forms and while it is functioning. The effective leader also is someone who is growing while also guiding the team. This is a person who knows that growth is never over; we're always strengthening and building some area of our lives.

The effective leader has learned to use time and location to her advantage. She doesn't just run at things, but is purposeful about what the team needs to accomplish and where team members need to grow personally and professionally. She, as an effective leader, needs to be alert to opportunities for instructing and training her team members to help them grow.

One of the responsibilities of a leader is seeing that team members have an opportunity for training. The training may be offered in a variety of ways:

- seminars
- workshops
- tapes to listen to and discuss at a later time
- books to read with an opportunity to share insights gained
- one-on-one time with someone who has the skills the team member needs to develop
- on-the-ground training with the team leader
- video-based training or programmed learning
- CBT (Computer-Based Training) or WBT (Web-Based Training) opportunities

THE TEAM LEADER

- phone coaching
- regular conference calls
- chat room opportunities

These are just a few suggestions. You need to evaluate the training that your people need and the type that would be most effective for the person or persons involved. You are responsible for seeing that your team members are trained.

Another concern of the effective leader is communication with team members. This type of leader creates an environment where one-on-one communication, effective listening, compassionate problem solving and encouragement are the norm rather than the exception. You need to see that developing people is your primary task, and this takes time. You can't develop people if you don't have time to spend with them observing, supporting and communicating.

Taking the time to build relationships will help improve your communication with team members. There are some relationship-building questions you can use to help you with this part of your responsibility.

- How can I communicate more effectively with this team member?
- What can I do to help this team member be more successful on the job?
- How can I support this member's efforts on the job?
- What can I provide that will increase productivity/service levels: equipment, materials or expertise?
- What can I do to help her develop professionally?
- Is there anything I can do to make the job more fun?
- What can I do to make/keep the relationship positive?

COACHING

Can you just imagine how it will revolutionize your relationship with team members when you start using these questions to help build a more positive relationship with them?

Issue of Motivation

As I pointed out in the last chapter, there is a discussion about what motivates people. And regardless of your stand on motivation, we know that all people need to be motivated and encouraged. There are a number of motivators, but the most effective ones require you as the leader to become involved with people on a personal level — you have to work with individuals! The most effective motivation builds the confidence and self-worth of the person being motivated.

Money is often considered to be the prime motivator for people on the job. For many people, the amount of money they are paid is a tool to help them measure how effectively they are doing their job. That's why when a person receives a bonus, a merit raise or a money award for a suggestion, it can be a motivator. The recognition of a job well done that comes with any one of those financial increases is as important as if not more important than the money itself. Although money may be seen as a powerful motivator, it is not necessarily the most effective one.

Praise is another form of motivation that people crave. Praise is that personal touch from the team leader that says, "I know you and appreciate your contributions to our team and our organization." Praise helps the team member feel good about herself and feeds the ego, which is vital if people are to be positively motivated.

Praise needs to be given for something specific in order for it to be most effective. It's even more powerful or effective when it's reserved for a special effort — something beyond the call of duty, so to speak. One of the best benefits of praise is that it reinforces positive behavior. Praise can be like rain to a desert when it falls on a team member who may be in a difficult situation but has managed to do one thing right. It helps the person feel valued and a necessary part of the team.

THE TEAM LEADER

Remember to praise for things that merit praise. Some team leaders are so busy praising every little thing that the praise becomes meaningless. Use the Burger Technique to effectively deliver praise.

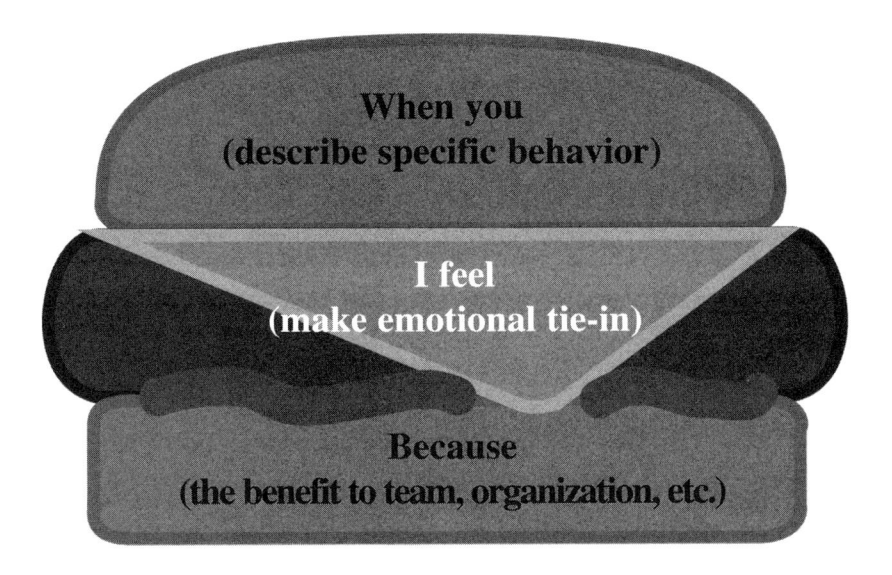

When you
(describe specific behavior)

I feel
(make emotional tie-in)

Because
(the benefit to team, organization, etc.)

Use the top bun to describe the specific behavior that you wish to draw attention to, the behavior that you want to praise. Then make the emotional tie-in that helps you connect with the person being praised. The "because" statement is an important part of the praise since it gives a specific benefit of the action. This helps your team member feel like she's more than just an insignificant person who has little or no real value to the team or the organization. An example of praise that uses the Burger Technique might sound something like this: "When you gathered all that information for our team meeting, I felt very proud of you for taking the initiative. That helped us make better decisions at the team meeting today because we had all the information we needed."

REFLECTIONS

Think for a moment about something one of your team members has done that gives you a reason for praising that member. Use the Burger Technique to write out your praise.

1. When you (specific behavior)

2. I feel (or felt) (emotions touched)

3. Because (specific benefit)

Reflections

The Team Leader

If at all possible you should praise in public. This encourages other team members and creates an atmosphere where praise and positive contributions are valued. When praise is delivered, you must be honest and sincere or you will sound phony, which builds an attitude of suspicion and destroys trust. If you don't honestly believe what you are saying, don't even bother. You will be damaging your team and your credibility. If you don't mean it, don't say it!

Lee Iacocca said, "When I must criticize somebody, I do it orally; when I praise somebody, I put it in writing." This can be a powerful way of delivering praise because the person can keep the written note or letter and read it over and over. When I am the team leader, I ask every team member to create a "Praise File." This is a place to keep all the written notes or letters of praise, development lists of training efforts and learning activities. What a great morale booster it is to go back and read through some of those when the day has been hectic or a team member begins to doubt abilities. This can be a great stress reducer because it helps to maintain perspective. Another valuable activity to ask the individuals on your team to do is to give you "Monday Notes." Every Monday morning, have your people give you a one-page report of last week's accomplishments and challenges. This will keep you alert for issues to praise, to probe or to monitor.

Recognition is another important motivational tool. People need recognition; it makes them feel valued and necessary. It is a powerful way of showing a team member that you care about the contributions she makes to the organization. Take time to address a person personally, asking about a project or activity she's involved in, offering support or help if there's a challenge (remember, no problems, only challenges, situations and opportunities) to be handled.

You need to know the personalities and needs of your team members in order to deliver the most effective recognition. Like feedback, it has to be tailored to the individual. Focus on the positive contributions the team member makes and give recognition for the good things the person has accomplished. This helps build a positive attitude in team members and increases the self-confidence that motivates them to be even more effective. It's a wonderful, continuous process that pays great dividends for both the

Coaching

team and the team member. You ultimately benefit because when your team members are successful, you as the team leader are perceived as being great with people. One of your goals is to bring out the best in others, and recognition is a powerful tool for achieving that

Another way to motivate your team members is to provide special awards in a formal recognition program specific to performance goals. This can be instituted just among the team members to recognize accomplishments that are above the norm for the organization. In a formal recognition program, the criteria for winning the awards are set forth, and everyone has the same opportunity to win the award.

Insights a Leader Must Possess

One of the insights an effective leader must possess is what makes people respond in different ways. There are basically four different response styles and a variety of assessment tools to identify the style of each person on the team. (See the SELF Profile, Appendix A, page 93). Knowing this helps you to be flexible in dealing with people and makes it possible for you to help each person use their natural abilities to make the team a success. This knowledge allows you to match tasks, recognition and awards to the style of each team member. Do you consciously consider factors that affect relationships in order to avoid the possible failure of that relationship? It is easy to respond to others the way you want people to respond to you. However, since we're not all the same, you need to think about what the other person needs from you so that both of you can be more successful.

Another insight is the value of evaluating what has or is taking place. Take the time to think about what you've learned from successes and learning experiences (sometimes called "failures"). We need to be willing and able to learn from the projects that are successfully completed. What made this project a success? What do we need to do to experience this success again? Is there anything we can do to be even more successful in the future?

THE TEAM LEADER

We should use evaluation to keep the team learning and growing together. Even if the project was not a success, we should still ask questions so we can learn from the experience. Success can be as valuable as failure as a learning tool if we take time to reflect on it. As Kouzes and Posner point out in *The Leadership Challenge*, "… even the most venturesome jobs will not help you grow if you do not take the time to reflect upon what you have learned from life's trials and errors. When we do recall in vivid detail, the people, the places, the events, the struggles, the victories — the very smell and texture of the action — we discover lasting lessons about how to more effectively lead others." Causing your team to evaluate realistically is one of your most powerful tools as a leader.

Another insight for a successful team leader is remembering that leadership is a two-way street. It's an exchange of ideas that allows the team to complete its tasks or reach its goal so the organization benefits tremendously from having this team. Remember, most employees in today's environment are well-informed and have lots of ideas and suggestions. Create an environment where the free exchange of ideas can take place and watch your team succeed. When your team succeeds, you succeed as a leader.

A six-step action plan can ensure that these insights occur. Whenever you gain a team member and/or whenever expectations change:

1. Ask the person what she considers good performance to be in the particular job.

2. Agree to the specific performance.

3. Ask how you and the person should keep score.

4. Regularly check or monitor the performance.

5. Provide consistent feedback.

6. Recycle. Start the process over whenever the job or team changes.

COACHING

Rethink Your Views of a Team

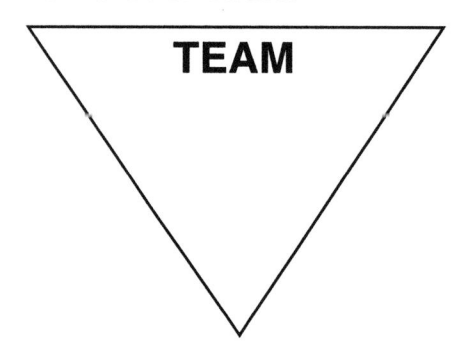

▽ **TEAM** ▽

    The leader knows that successful teams are the ones that have the broadest powers to function and accomplish their tasks. This leader is one who empowers her team members. The more the team members are empowered, the larger the power base becomes. This empowerment moves up and down the inverted triangle (shown above) — the more empowered the team becomes, the more empowered the team leader becomes. Leaders and team members are willing to influence one another. The key to this empowered team becomes cooperation, not competition.

Values, Characteristics of an Effective Leader

    An effective leader values the people on her team and looks for ways to let those team members know they are valued. She encourages team members to take advantage of their strengths and helps members continue to build those strengths. The leader is willing to invest herself in the lives of others and is excited when team members are successful.

    The effective leader is also a person of integrity. She knows that people will not follow someone they do not trust, so she is honest and true in dealing with her team members. They know that when she gives her word on something, it will be done. If she tells a team member, "I'll check into it," that person knows she really will check it out. She does what it takes to remember what she tells people so she can follow up.

The Team Leader

A leader makes change a part of the team's expectations and experiences. Successful leaders are change agents. They don't fight change but promote an atmosphere of flexibility personally and for the team. This is a leader who values the risk takers on the team. When there is an atmosphere of change and risk taking, the team members feel free to think outside the box. This is the team that will come up with new, innovative ways of completing the task.

A leader must be competent in what she does. She is building her interpersonal skills as well as keeping her technical skills current. She is a person who values and practices lifelong learning and personal growth. Because of this belief, she encourages her team members to continue their professional and personal growth. She is building up individuals as well as strengthening the organization.

Successful leaders are optimistic. They believe in the organization, the team and the task. They believe that the future holds a wonderful promise and naturally share this optimism with team members. This encourages the team to greater productivity and also increases the morale of the work force.

Good leaders are also committed — to the task, to the organization and, most of all, to the team members. This commitment is what makes it possible for the leader to invest in others. This commitment also spills over into the way the team functions. Because of the leader's commitment, team members will be more willing to invest themselves to accomplish the goals of the team. When this occurs, the organization benefits with increased productivity, customer service, etc.

The successful leader can articulate the vision and stay focused on that vision. This is the gathering point for the team. The vision gives the team purpose, direction and enthusiasm for the tasks. Vision is what makes it possible for team members to see beyond just a list of tasks. Because of the vision given and re-emphasized by the leader, team members are able to see the big picture. People are willing to invest themselves when they're given a vision. Help them get in touch with energy and initiative they aren't aware of by clearing roadblocks and smoothing the path ahead of them.

COACHING

In John Maxwell's book *Developing the Leader Within You*, he lists "seven deadly sins" that excellent leaders avoid:

1. Trying to be liked rather than respected
2. Not asking team members for advice and help
3. Thwarting personal talent by emphasizing rules rather than skills
4. Not keeping criticism constructive
5. Not developing a sense of responsibility in team members
6. Treating everyone the same way
7. Failing to keep people informed

As you look over this list, which one is the most relevant for you as a leader? Put a check mark by that one and keep it in mind as you think about steps you want to take to build your skills as a leader. Consider the following information as you think about how to deal with these issues.

Trying to be liked rather than respected generally occurs because of the personality of the leader. Some leaders want everyone to like them. They find it difficult to operate in an environment where they need to be respected rather than liked as a person. (If you have taken the SELF Profile – see Appendix A, page 93 – you are an "L," a relationship-focused individual, and the Profile has some tips for working with other response styles.) This can also occur as a result of low self-esteem. Your job is to identify the cause of this feeling and begin to change it, remembering respect is a basic necessity of leading effectively.

Communication will handle deadly sins two and seven. The fear of asking team members for advice may be because of the leader's lack of confidence in her job skills or capabilities. Failing to keep people informed and not asking them for help or advice make team members feel unappreciated or not valued. Working on the interpersonal skills of communication and listening will help correct either one of these situations.

THE TEAM LEADER

Not keeping criticism constructive is also a communication problem. Some people don't have any trouble communicating, they just have trouble phrasing it in a positive fashion. Practice saying things in a positive way. Look for the best way to state things. Some people can even say positive things in a negative way that wipes out the value of what is being said.

When the leader relies too heavily on the rules rather than utilizing the skills of team members, the team becomes stifled in accomplishing the task. Flexibility is a key attribute of most successful leaders. You as a leader need to build your ability to take risks and try things in a new and different way. This flexibility will strengthen your team's ability to get the job done — regardless!

Empower your people by letting them have responsibility. Give them the support they need to be successful and then let go of your team! People who feel empowered have a highly developed sense of responsibility and want to see the team succeed. When the team succeeds, you as the leader succeed.

Treating everyone the same way is a mistake because people are different. You'll have some team members who need more guidance and direction than other members. Some members of the team work best when they know what needs to be done, when, and who is responsible for what. Turn them loose and watch the team succeed when the members are encouraged, trained, valued and given clear direction. This can happen when you are fair with your team members. This doesn't mean that you treat everyone exactly the same.

Summary

In this chapter we've looked at what an effective leader does and the responsibilities she has for her team members. We've also looked at the issues of motivation and motivators the team leader can use to help her team achieve even greater heights. In order for the leader to have a successful team, there are insights a leader most possess, such as how to use evaluation as a tool to keep the team focused and motivated. The leader has to remember that people are different and need to be handled differently. Another insight is that

COACHING

leadership is a two-way street. When these insights are combined with the inverted-triangle view of the team, the leader has some powerful tools to use. Even when all these insights and understandings are in place, the leader needs to have some specific values and characteristics so the team can follow the leader with confidence and enthusiasm. Leaders are made, not born, and every person has skills and abilities that can be developed into leadership qualities. How much you develop is something that you and you alone can control.

— *Coach Joe Says ...*

It was a blessing when my wife and I attended a seminar "Love is a Decision" by Dr. Gary Smalley. We were asked during the seminar to share the one thing that we admired most about each other. My wife said, "You love to learn." I said, "You always find the good in others." Learning and praising can happen at the same time.

Rick Warren, author and extraordinary team leader, said, "The moment you stop learning, you stop leading." Never stop learning. It's your secret weapon for success.

REFLECTIONS

1. What leadership behavior will best guarantee increased performance from your team?

2. What barrier could hold you back?

3. How can you overcome the challenges?

Reflections

Coaching

3 A COACHING MODEL

In previous chapters, we looked at what makes an effective team and some characteristics of an effective team leader. However, an effective leader knows that different situations require the leader to respond in different ways.

Sometimes the leader needs to function as a coach, which means helping the team or team members build job skills. An example of this is the coach who helps the team develop the discipline to be effective and achieve its goals. Likewise, the coach who develops speaking skills and the ability to relate precisely to others pushes himself to greater accomplishment.

Another role of the leader is to be a mentor to individuals on the team. The mentor is someone who provides instruction by example. The leader in the mentor role is looking for opportunities to help each member of the team build skills and become more of a successful team member. The mentoring leader is also looking for potential leaders to develop.

The third role a leader has to assume is to counsel team members who aren't performing to an acceptable level.

In this chapter, we'll take a closer look at a coaching model you can use to be more effective as a coach by helping your team build job skills and performance.

COACHING

What Is the Model?

National Seminars' model for successful coaching is called the Five-Step Staff Coaching Model. It starts with a realistic assessment of the current performance level of each team member. You must know whether each team member is functioning at an acceptable level, above the standard or below the standard. You'll have to spend some time getting to know your people if you're going to realistically assess them.

You'll need to discover the obvious strengths and weaknesses of each team member along with understanding their basic responsibilities. To accomplish this, examine each task the person is performing to determine the person's performance level. Use predetermined, consistent and qualitative measures. Also examine the strengths of the person to see whether another assignment would fit his strengths better. Take into consideration the work history of this person. Is your current assessment of the person in line with his work history, with the organization and with other teams on which he has served? You can't set your team up for success if you don't take the time to assess where the individual team members are currently.

One way to assess your team members is through personal observation. This requires a face-to-face discussion to help you know what motivates the team member. You'll also have an opportunity to find out how he feels about the tasks he's performing and what goals he has for his future.

You might want to use a series of questions to help you with the face-to-face assessment. Modify the following questions to help you get to know your team members better.

1. What do you like best about your job?

2. What do you like least about your job?

3. What has satisfied you most about your job performance in recent months?

4. What has frustrated you most about project duties?

A Coaching Model

5. What do you feel you contribute best as a member of our team?
6. What changes have you recommended in your job over the past year?
7. What training has best prepared you to do what you do?
8. Are there aspects of your job for which you feel unequipped in any way?
9. What is the one area of your job in which you would like to improve?

These questions were taken from *The Manager's Role as Coach*, a National Seminars training manual, and will help you understand what motivates your team member, what goals the team member has, and what problem areas or lack of training he feels is keeping him from being a successful member of the team. In addition, these questions will give you insight into the successes that the member feels he has experienced recently. Questioning is a key skill for coaches.

After you have completed the face-to-face interview, be sure to write down your impressions and any other ideas that you may have after the meeting is over. This helps you keep an accurate record of what took place. You can then use this information to develop plans for strengthening this team member. Also, as you observe the team member on the job, you'll have other ideas about what he needs from you as the team leader.

You should also take time to review performance evaluations and listen to any insights other team leaders may have about this team member. Remember to consider this type of information only in the context of your observations about the team member. Circumstances may have changed, the team member's assignments may be more in line with his abilities and interests, or even a change in team membership can influence the type of job a team member is doing.

Another tool you might want to consider is a talent survey that the team member fills out about himself. This written format would simply be another way for you to gain insight into how the team member views the talents and abilities he brings to the team.

Once the assessment is completed for each team member, you are ready to use the Five-Step Staff Coaching Model to lead your team to success. The value of the Five-Step Staff Coaching Model is that you're able to start where you are and move toward a more successful team with an organized plan. Things aren't left to chance, but move in an orderly fashion to help each team member achieve at a higher level. That benefits the team member, the organization and you as a leader.

The Five-Step Staff Coaching Model

Once you know the performance level of your team members, you can decide which of the three coaching roles you need to use — coach, mentor or counselor.

If your team member is functioning above the standard set for your team's performance, use your mentoring role to help this team member grow. If the performance is standard, what will you do to encourage that person to grow and build his strengths? You'll use the coaching role to help the team member develop above-standard performance. This benefits both the member and the team because people love to be part of a winning team. Also, when one team member experiences success, other team members are encouraged. They begin to think, "If he can do it, I can too!" Remember the old adage, "Nothing succeeds like success."

If the performance is below standard, then you will need to function in your counselor role to bring the team member's performance up to standard. This is vital because members who don't perform their functions and bring their best efforts to the team weaken the team. They tend to drag the performance of the whole team down over time. Team members may begin to develop the attitude that "it doesn't really matter," and then they stop giving their best effort to the team.

A Coaching Model

The five-step coaching model is designed to help you, as the coach, encourage and equip your team members to achieve higher performance levels. It gives you a tool to help each team member give his best to the team. This builds self-esteem and confidence in your team members. It also prepares them for promotions and career advancement.

Leadership Behaviors in the Model

If you're going to be effective, your team has to believe in you as a leader and coach. There are four different leadership behaviors in this coaching model that will make you more effective. The first focuses on building involvement and trust with your team. Members learn to trust you when you are involved with them. Author Tom Peters coined the phrase "management by walking around," which means the leader is among the team members. This helps the leader know what is really going on. It also helps the team see the leader as someone who is really involved, not just talking about being involved with the team. The benefit of this is that team members see the leader as caring and approachable. The leader isn't stuck in some office rarely seen by team members, but is someone they know on a first-name basis. Because of this familiarity, the coach often discovers information that helps him be more effective leading the team. Team members find it easier to respect and trust the leader who isn't afraid to get involved with them.

The leader also must clarify and verify what needs to be done and who will do it. Team members require a clear understanding of their roles on the team. They know what they must do and when it has to be done. The leader also enables team members to support and help each other. The leader reviews action plans the team has for achieving its goals, clarifies misunderstandings and affirms the direction of the team.

Being able to affirm and acknowledge is another behavior the effective leader must assume. The leader is looking for situations where a team member is successful. The leader then affirms the effort and encourages the member to continue the productive behavior. In this role, the leader may need to give some warnings and reminders and remain visible. Because of this visibility and support, team members feel valued and trusted by their leader.

COACHING

The successful coach is able to motivate and inspire the team. He challenges members to achieve more and supports the team in its effort to strive for greater accomplishments. Even when things aren't so positive, the coach still encourages the team and pushes it to continue trying. The coach keeps the team focused on possibilities for success in the future and reminders of successes in the past. The leader knows that team members are motivated by different things and matches the motivation to the individual.

To Develop, Support and Grow a Team

To develop a successful team, a leader must establish a solid foundation. There are several qualities that are necessary to build that foundation, and one of them is flexibility. Since the team is constantly changing in some way, you need to be flexible and able to grow in your leadership abilities. If you expect your team members to be flexible, to change and to grow, then you must model that quality for them. Like any other quality, skill or trait, this can be developed. One technique to develop flexibility is to plan to do one thing differently each day. Note some activity you always do a certain way and do it differently. Cultivate openness.

Another quality for the effective leader is being willing to help your team achieve its goals. You must be willing to get into the middle of the action and help your team members. One of your jobs is to help your team members succeed individually and as a team. When your team members know they can count on you to pitch in during the tough times, they'll be more likely to give their very best efforts to the task. You have set the stage, blazed the trail and shown them what is expected of every team member, even the team leader. What is important here is noting their goal — not yours.

You also need to show caring and understanding for your team members. This means you're willing to let these people be human. You will expect them to achieve great things as a team and as individuals. You'll also expect them to make mistakes. When mistakes happen, you'll be there as a support to help the team find solutions and solve the problems those mistakes created. That's helping your team members develop the problem-solving skills that will help

A Coaching Model

them both personally and professionally. How? Bite back the critique and focus on alternative ways to solve problems.

Think about how you communicate with your team. Do you let the team members feel involved in team tasks? Do you help the team move toward the successful completion of the tasks it has been assigned? Is it possible for the team to excel and receive recognition when it completes the assigned tasks? Would you want to work for a boss like you? These are all questions to ask yourself as you evaluate your communication with the team and its members.

Learn to use powerful words of encouragement. Words like "great," "excellent," "exceptional," "wonderful," and "outstanding" give life and energy to conversations. This in turn begins to influence your team members. They start to feel more energy and interest in being part of this team. Remember the principle of "act as if!" Even if you don't feel very enthusiastic or energetic, act as if you do. It's an interesting phenomenon that our feelings will follow our actions. This influences your team tremendously, so act as if you are feeling positive and enthusiastic all the time. This may be a challenge. Many people feel they are not "optimistic." You need not change your personality. Do change your verbal behaviors.

Listening is another important part of communicating effectively and developing your team. Effective leaders learn to listen to what the speaker is saying. This means you're not thinking ahead or jumping to conclusions, but you're making a conscious effort to hear what the person is really saying. Listen not only with your ears but also with your eyes. What is their body language saying? Do their facial expressions send a different message? Listen to the whole message and then clarify. This is a skill you must constantly practice and consciously develop. To increase listening, use audio tapes, count to five before responding, and ask more "and then what?" questions.

COACHING

Be aware of your own body language and facial expressions. What are you communicating with your face? Do you look bored and uninterested or do you appear interested and concerned? Are you drumming your fingers, fidgeting with something on your desk or generally being inattentive to the team member? Is it easy for your team members to talk to you? Non-verbal communications can sabotage any effort. Videotape yourself. Note facial tendencies. Pay attention to eye contact as you are listening. Note your body posture. Are you open or closed in appearance?

Being good at giving feedback is another sign of an effective coach. Both verbally and in writing, let people know how they're doing. When a project has been completed, send a note to team members thanking them for their part in the project. Compliment the team publicly in front of your boss or other team leaders. Use a team meeting to express your appreciation to the team. Send a letter to your boss outlining the team's success and make sure every team member receives a copy. Let your people know you believe in them and are proud of their accomplishments. When giving feedback, it's very important to be positive in the way the feedback is presented. Even when dealing with a team that failed or didn't achieve the expected results, be positive in how you deal with the learning experience. A good rule to remember is, "Be soft on people, hard on facts." This does not negate the need to be honest, specific and focused. Remember, feedback is about what the individual did — not what you think or how you would do it.

Successful coaches also provide encouragement for the team and its members. You will be alert for opportunities for the team to be successful. You want your team to succeed and you want team members to feel they are vital to that success. Even if a task wasn't successfully completed, compliment team members for their effort, their abilities, or their willingness to stick with the task even through tough times. Skill is required here not to minimize acceptable performance.

Another aspect of successfully developing a team is the ability to be proactive rather than reactive to situations. Thinking ahead and anticipating problems so the team can come up with alternatives is the sign of a proactive coach or leader. This also means you're making things happen and setting the stage for your team to successfully complete the tasks it has been given. To be

A Coaching Model

proactive requires planning skills, so the team leader must develop excellent planning skills.

Being open and honest with your team members is another important part of growing a team. Share as much with your team members as you can because this makes them feel like they're a valuable part of the organization. When your team members trust you to build them up and give them opportunities to excel, they are inspired to even greater efforts. This makes you and the organization winners — but the greatest benefit is the growth you see in your team members. A coach is a builder of people, and as a result, you are seen as a successful coach who gets the very best results from any team you're leading.

Two other qualities that successful team leaders often exhibit is humor and spontaneity. The ability to laugh at yourself sets the stage for others to laugh with you. Humor lets people deal with their mistakes and problems in a more effective way. It reduces stress and relieves tension. It is a means for connecting. When people are able to laugh, they have a sense of calmness and control even though things may be careening madly out of control. When team members aren't panicking, they are able to use their very best abilities to solve problems and deal with conflicts. Humor can be the tool to help that happen. Be spontaneous in celebrations. Have a surprise ice cream party by bringing in ice cream bars for everyone on the team. Take the team out to lunch. Even if each team member pays for his own lunch, the time together will pay great dividends. Celebrate birthdays. Let your team know you value humor and spontaneity in the team.

When to Cheer

You as a leader need to believe that your team can accomplish the impossible (or at least next to impossible). When you have those types of expectations for the team, you're able to stretch team members to the maximum, and this accelerates personal and professional growth. This, in turn, spurs your team members to greater creativity — new ways of looking at old situations or processes. This occurs when the team leader is involved in cheering and encouraging the team.

COACHING

You need to cheer and encourage your team when things are not going well. This doesn't mean you are a Pollyanna and ignoring reality. Lead the team to look objectively at why a project is behind schedule or not achieving the results the team expected. Remember, it's all in how you approach the situation. Effective team leaders learn how to cheer the team on even in difficult situations.

You function as a motivator for the team and this builds members' self-esteem and confidence. It also builds a bridge between you and team members. You are open to communication from team members and encourage them to share information and ideas with you as team leader and with the rest of the team. When you're cheering your team on, you can still offer suggestions and evaluation so you're not abdicating your role as leader. You're expanding your role as leader to include encouragement and support.

— *Coach Joe Says ...*

Frank Murphy, CEO for three hospitals in Tampa, FL, is called "Coach Frank" by his staff. Being at one of his staff meetings has the excitement of an Amway meeting. The cheerleader helps set the tone of enthusiasm and excitement about what the team is accomplishing.

What It Means to Lead

It has been said, "Success is not established by how high we climb ... but by how many people we take with us as we climb." Coaches who lead are willing to invest themselves in the people they are leading. You will be successful as a coach if you make other people on your team successful. There are times when you will need to lead your team members to achieve greater success. As a result, the entire team will succeed.

A COACHING MODEL

When you inspire your team with the vision of what it can accomplish as a team, you are leading. But you can't take the team where you haven't gone yourself. All of the qualities that are required of a coach and the foundation you build with your people determine whether or not your team will follow you. A leader must have followers, and followers today are very smart and talented. They won't follow a leader who lacks integrity, isn't concerned about them as individuals, and won't put himself at risk for the team.

Why People Don't Do What They Are Supposed to Do

There are a wide variety of reasons why people don't do what they are supposed to do. However, when you look carefully, you'll find some basic issues that seem to surface about job performance. Today's team members are generally more knowledgeable about their work situation than the work force in years past. Yet, with all their knowledge and expertise, they may not know how to do the job. Remember, just because the team member has been told how to do the job doesn't mean he knows how to do it. One of your roles as coach is to see that training occurs and that it is effective training. Always evaluate the effectiveness of the training. (See Table, Appendix B, page 105, "Why People Don't Do What They're Supposed to Do.")

Team members feel they have certain rights and expectations that must be met if they are going to be a vital part of the team. Because of their attitudes and expectations, some people don't do what they are supposed to do because they don't know why they should do it. It's not enough for the team leader to tell the team what needs to be done. You must paint the big picture and then show your team how they are a vital part of this bigger picture.

Some team members won't do what they're supposed to do because they think they have a better idea or that your idea won't work. You must set the stage for innovative thinking and be open to possibilities. This is also the time to coach your team members to examine the suggested solution carefully to see if it is a valid option.

COACHING

Use the following four steps to evaluate suggested solutions:

- Examine the suggestion or idea. What is the real issue?

- Has something like this been successfully done before? What are some other options we could consider?

- What are the consequences of each option suggested? The consequences must be considered because that helps you decide which solution will be best.

- Select the best solution based on the real issue, the possible options and the consequences of each option.

This is where your team has the possibility of really shining. When the team moves into this type of problem solving, the energy and creativity begin to flow. This becomes encouraging and exciting to team members and can lead them to make an even greater commitment to the team and its tasks.

Team members may not do what they're supposed to do because they misunderstand and think they are doing it. Or perhaps they think something else is more important. Use feedback to make sure your team members are on track and that they understand the priorities. Keep the big picture before them and emphasize their team's importance in achieving the big picture. This will help members know where they should be investing their time and energy.

These are some of the common reasons why team members don't do what they are supposed to do. One of your responsibilities as the coach is to discover the reason your team member isn't fulfilling his role. Then work with him to overcome the reason so he can make his contribution to the team as a whole.

Summary

Successful coaches are seen as caring about team members. The role of the coach is to develop those team members so the team can accomplish its tasks. It's more than just getting the job done, though. It's also equipping and building your team members so they are more successful both personally and professionally. This is an investment in the future.

A Coaching Model

— *Coach Joe Says ...*

A coach must see his people as his greatest asset. Developing people is the highest calling of a coach.

A coach should be constantly building the foundational qualities that make him a great coach. He recognizes and is able to clearly define what needs to be done, encourages his team, motivates and inspires his team, and most of all, he is involved with his team. He cannot coach from a distance; he must be in the everyday life of his team.

As an effective coach, you are also aware of the reasons team members don't always do what they're supposed to do. You take this knowledge and move to equip your team members to achieve and accomplish not only team goals, but also personal goals. This builds a more effective organization and more powerful teams. You are successfully and effectively filling your role as a coach.

John Madden, who for years coached the Oakland Raiders, said, "I didn't want a big play once in a while, I wanted a solid play every time." One of Madden's strengths was taking players no other team could control or use effectively. He used his coaching skills to build highly successful teams by developing the players on his team. He built teams that gave solid plays, game after game. When you help your team give solid plays day after day, you will be a highly successful coach.

REFLECTIONS

Which quality do you need to develop more fully in order to build your skills as a successful coach?

What are three actions you can take to help you build that quality?

1.

2.

3.

What are some other ways you can be spontaneous with your team? List at least four below:

1.

2.

3.

4.

Reflections

4 "COACHING" THE TEAM

To be an effective team coach you must want to help the team members grow, expand and become more tomorrow than they are today. In other words, you want to help people develop. If you don't have that desire and you aren't willing to get involved in the lives of your team members, coaching will be a difficult, if not impossible, task for you. As a coach, you will be in a position to see growth and advancement for the people you're coaching.

Coaching is invaluable because there are only three ways you can affect performance: change the worker, the work or the workplace. Coaching supports the worker.

The Coach's Role With a Team

Your role as a coach is to give clarification of performance expectations. Let your team members know what they are expected to achieve and then give them the tools to be successful. This may require a change in the team member's point of view. The member may have felt that the effort given to the team was more than adequate, even if the results weren't what you expected or even what the team expected. In that case, you need to help the team member change her point of view about what is acceptable or you may need to help the member change her point of view about the team's task or objective. Sometimes people have wrong ideas or they've made wrong assumptions, and no one takes the time to clarify or help them understand.

COACHING

An effective coach builds a team that is self-sufficient and autonomous. This doesn't mean that the team leader is no longer necessary, but means that she's building a team of people who can think for themselves. When that happens, she's free to spend more time on the big picture and less on the details. The coach can then lead the team to even greater achievement because she's being proactive rather than always reacting to current situations.

It is important to gain insight into the behavior and feelings of team members. You can help team members understand each other's response style and how best to work together. These style differences are positive for the team once the team knows how to effectively use the information. Give the team time to get to know more about each other. Use a tool like the SELF Profile to help build an appreciation for diversity of team members. (See Appendix A, page 93.)

The team that has an effective coach has the ability to accept more difficult tasks. As skills are developed and abilities utilized, team members begin to feel that together they can tackle almost anything. Team members continue to build their skills as they sharpen problem-solving abilities, decision-making abilities, communication skills and consensus-building skills. These are all skills that help team members become a more effective part of the organization.

What Does It Mean to Coach a Team?

When you coach a team you help develop people. You help team members build job skills while growing their interpersonal skills also. At the first football practice of each season, Vince Lombardi would say to his team, "Gentlemen, this is a football." These were men who had played football for years, and yet their coach knew how important it was to master the basics. Unfortunately, we can be sloppy about the basics. Often we want to rush ahead and try new things without having a firm foundation built on basic job skills. An important behavior is to regularly remind your team of the basics often enough that it is able to build on these basics successfully. Periodically review the basics with your team.

"Coaching" the Team

Keep the team focused on the goal or tasks it has been given. Teams will tend to pursue goals other than the ones given by the organization. The other goal may seem more exciting or may offer more visibility to the team. The coach keeps reminding the members of the goal the team has been given.

Coaches also help teams know how to use the diversity of the team members to accomplish the goal. Each team member has strengths and abilities. The coach helps the team utilize these abilities and minimize the weaknesses of team members. In a well-balanced team, the strength of one member will compensate for the weakness of another member. That's one of the values of teams — each person is able to be successful in her own way.

Clarify the Role of Coach

You will need to go into the coach model when team members' skills need to be strengthened. The coaching can take place one-on-one with team members or with the whole team. If the coaching will benefit the whole team, get all members involved. If the skill to be developed is needed by only one or two team members, some personal coaching time is in order.

It is the responsibility of the leader to create the atmosphere and opportunity for coaching. Don't wait for the team member to come to you. Seek her out and create the coaching environment. When you are a successful leader, you must maintain absolute confidentiality. This is vital for a leader, because if you violate confidentiality, you've destroyed the trust of your team members. When that trust is destroyed, it's almost impossible to rebuild.

Team members expect their coach to be supportive of them. This means even if they are wrong, you will stand behind them (and not so far behind that they can't see you). When the team is gathered you can deal with your disappointment in the results, but support your team in public. This gives your team courage to try new things, to be creative and innovative. Knowing that you're supportive gives the team courage to take risks, and when risks are taken some amazing things occur. Think how many things would have never been discovered and how different our lives would have been if someone before us hadn't been willing to take a risk. Set the stage for your team members to take a risk! Most learning comes from studying the why of a mistake.

See that team members are rewarded for accomplishments and performance. That doesn't always mean more money. Remember, praise and recognition are two of the greatest rewards people can receive. Be free with your praise, but be honest with it also. Don't go around giving recognition for every little thing that is done. On the other hand, don't neglect to recognize when a team's accomplishments are outstanding. Maybe the result wasn't outstanding, but the effort was more than you expected. Give recognition for the effort because this keeps the team from becoming discouraged. Don't focus on what's wrong, but on what's right. "Eighty-five percent of this project was just what we needed. Now what can we do to correct the other 15 percent?" is an example of focusing on what's right and moving toward a solution to the problem.

Match the need of the team member to the type of coaching that will be most beneficial. However, always be consistent in dealing with the team. That gives the team confidence in your ability to lead. The team members know where they stand with the coach who is consistent — no guessing games here. "What you see is what you get," Flip Wilson said.

The Coach Is a Hands-On Leader

Be a hands-on coach. The coach is someone who is involved with the team. The coach doesn't usually play but is always on the sidelines, ready and available during the entire game. Coaches don't disappear when it is time for the team to perform. They are right there watching the game, shouting encouragement, giving suggestions, offering ideas for improvement, and reminding the team of strategies for winning.

— *Coach Joe Says ...*

The coach inspires the team members and challenges them to reach their highest potential as part of the team.

"Coaching" the Team

This is not a person who is hiding in the coaching office waiting to hear how the game went. This is an individual who's in the middle of what's going on. The hands-on coach is committed to helping this team be the very best team possible. This doesn't happen from a distance, so if you are going to be a successful coach, you've got to be with the team.

The Team in Which the Leader Sees Some Potential

Every team has potential, and through coaching you develop that potential. As coach, you know what needs to be done to help the team grow. This will involve many of the things already mentioned in this book, such as assessing the team members' abilities and making plans to strengthen those abilities so the team can enjoy success. When a team begins to experience success, it becomes even more successful. Everyone enjoys being on a winning team, so your role as a coach is to build a winning team even if it hasn't been successful before now.

Often teams that haven't experienced success feel isolated from the team leader or discouraged at the lack of involvement from their leader. It will require a consistent and constant commitment on your part as the coach to help the team become successful. You must be willing to make that investment of time and energy if you're going to build a winning team. Use your best interpersonal skills and team-building strategies to create an atmosphere so the team is able to accomplish the tasks and goals it has been given and become a winning team. To sum up all motivational theories: People want to be winners, and people want to be part of a winning team.

— *Coach Joe Says ...*

I remember George, who was a participant in a seminar I did for a power company. Months later at another session, George presented to me a copy of one of his college textbooks. He had returned to school after being inspired in the first seminar. The title of the book was *The Leader of the Future*. In the front was written, "Thanks for reviving in me the need to improve myself. George."

COACHING

Why Is the Role of Coach Beneficial?

Coaching is beneficial because it helps the team stay focused, brings out the best in the team members, and leads the team to create strategies for getting the job done. Coaching sets the team up for success by motivating the members to strive for higher achievement. Coaching helps the team overcome obstacles that it might face and encourages it to stay with the job until it's done and done successfully.

Goal — New Levels of Performance

The reason to coach a team is to help that team achieve new levels of performance. Teams left on their own will usually never achieve the high levels of performance of which they are capable. They need coaches to give encouragement and direction. Since the coach is involved in building people or team members, the coach is always urging higher levels of performance. The coach has to be careful not to discourage team members by pushing too hard or expecting too much from the team. However, the coach also needs to remember that many performance barriers in sports have been broken when a committed coach and committed athlete worked together. The four-minute mile and the 500-pound mark in weight lifting are just two examples. Once the four-minute mile was broken, several runners broke it in a short time because they had seen it could be done. The weight lifter couldn't lift more than 498 pounds until his coach fooled him by telling him the bar was only 498 pounds when it was really 501 pounds. Once he had successfully lifted 501 pounds in practice, he was able to repeat the performance in competition. The coach can make or break the athlete. The same is true for the team. You, as the coach, have tremendous power and influence on the team. Give members your best effort, and you will see fantastic results.

Why Some Leaders Don't Coach

"I don't have time" is the number one reason leaders give for not coaching. They feel coaching takes too long for both the leader and the team member. A

"COACHING" THE TEAM

good question to ask yourself is, "If I don't have time now to help this team member be successful, will I have time later to invest in dealing with the problems created because of lack of information or skills to handle the task correctly?" This question can help put things in perspective for the leader who feels that there's not enough time to coach.

Some leaders hesitate to coach because they don't want team members to feel like they aren't trusted. As a leader, it is your job to see that team members know how to handle tasks effectively. This means you will be involved in coaching members and letting them know your expectations. Spend time with team members, communicate freely with them, and they will feel valued and trusted. They will welcome the skills you bring to the task of coaching.

There are leaders who think that team members "will contact me if they need help." Some people are hesitant to ask for information or help because they don't want to be seen as incompetent or unable to perform tasks. These people need to see and hear that you encourage communication and questions. Be careful never to penalize a team member who asks for help or more information. They need to know that you value your role as a coach and want to help them. They also need to know that you see a major part of your success as helping the whole team be successful.

Some leaders don't feel comfortable in the coaching role. "I don't really know how to coach," is their excuse. The good news is, coaching is a skill that you can develop and strengthen — no one is born knowing how to be an excellent coach. Or the leader may fall into the trap of thinking that coaching is the job of the organization's trainer. Training is valuable, but isn't the cure-all for every situation. The lack of productivity or inability to work as a team may be a direct result of the leader's style, communication patterns or other interpersonal problems. This needs to be handled by the leader functioning in the coaching role.

One other reason leaders don't coach is they don't feel like it's really all that important. "I've got other more important things to do," may be the leader's attitude. Since the leader's success is dependent on the team and its

COACHING

members, the leader needs to provide all the support, guidance and direction possible. It's difficult to see how there could be a better way to spend time than by helping people grow, develop and become more successful. Coaching sets up a potential win-win environment for you and your team members. This is coaching at its very best.

Pitfalls

There are pitfalls that will undermine your team and set it up for failure. One thing that will lead to disaster for you as a coach and for your team is to exaggerate the behavior of a team member or exaggerate a situation. Be aware of generalizing when you're talking to your team members. Watch your vocabulary for "absolute" words such as "never," "always," "everybody," "no one" and "all the time." Your team members know that "everybody let the team down" is an exaggeration. A statement like, "You never get your part of the project right" demeans the individual and offers no constructive value. Be very specific when dealing with team members and avoid generalizations.

Another pitfall is assuming that the employee knows the problem and the solution. If you assume she knows the problem and the solution, she will be hesitant to come to you for clarification and guidance. The act of assuming closes the door to effective communication, so be open and available to your team members. Talk to them, listen to them, and communicate with them. If there's a misunderstanding, take responsibility for the misunderstanding and concentrate on communicating more clearly. Take time with your team members to open the lines of communication. Not hearing what your team members have to offer is definitely a pitfall for a coach.

Before someone can know what is not good performance, they must know what is. Clearly state what is acceptable performance. Give a picture to the person: This is what is expected; it looks like, sounds like, feels like this. Make it quantifiable.

Since we're looking at opening the lines of communication, let's examine another pitfall: talking at your team members, not with them. Start using collective pronouns such as "we," "our" and "us." These words can build a

"Coaching" the Team

sense of "we're all in this together" and encourage your team members to stay committed to the team, the task and you as the team leader. Only when they have the sense that you're part of the team will they be motivated to perform beyond minimum expectations.

Talking about attitudes and not talking about behavior can be self-defeating for a coach. When you talk about attitudes, you're attacking the person at the very core of her self-esteem. When you talk about a person's attitude, she generally goes into the defensive mode. This makes it difficult, if not impossible, for the team member to hear what you're really saying. It's difficult to separate fact from fiction when dealing with attitudes. When you deal specifically with behavior, it's easy to point out a solution to the situation. You're dealing with hard facts rather than emotions, so there's less need for the team member to go into the defensive mode.

When you neglect to follow up with your team members, you'll end up being surprised. Sometimes it's not a pleasant surprise! Instead of giving a project with only a final due date, set some checkpoints along the way. This will help the team member set goals, plan the use of time carefully, and let you know about problems or possible missed deadlines before the end of the project. You can then help the team member make alternate plans to get the task completed on time or look for other solutions.

One more pitfall for a coach is failing to notice and reward behavior that is improving or has improved. Fortunately, it is easy to reward people because they love recognition. When a team leader notices achievement and gives recognition for it, the team member becomes more motivated. When a team member is motivated, she is able to achieve more. Her creative juices begin to flow, her energy level rises, and she has a "can do" attitude. This in turn helps the team to be more motivated. These are all positives for you as a team leader also.

Any of these pitfalls will demoralize your team members. Demoralized team members aren't able to function at their best, and so the team suffers, the organization suffers, and you as a coach suffer. It is so easy to fall into some of these common pitfalls. Be alert for opportunities to build your team members and avoid these pitfalls.

Communicating as a Coach

When you are in the coaching role, you will need to communicate effectively with the team. That means you'll take time to be sure your team members know what you expect from them. You will need to talk about the vision, the direction and the tasks of the team. You'll make sure there's clarity about these expectations and that team members understand the part they play in accomplishing the goals. Make sure you avoid industry jargon when talking with your team. Also eliminate abbreviations, nicknames and acronyms from your vocabulary. This automatically cuts out the person who doesn't know or has forgotten the meanings of them. Barriers are built when we act like everyone knows what we're talking about. It's simply a good idea to communicate in clear, simple, everyday language to cut down on misunderstandings.

When you're talking with your team members, create an environment that is distraction-free. Eliminate unnecessary noise and pick your meeting areas carefully so everyone can hear and see what is happening. Use current stories, show examples or give a demonstration to help clarify your message. Because we are all easily distracted, the more hooks you can use to involve the listener in the message, the more likely it will be that the message will be heard.

Get your thoughts and information organized before you start to communicate. This is true whether you're communicating in person, over the phone or in writing. The shorter the message, the easier it will be for people to remember. However, be sure to include all the details your team will need to successfully complete the task. Make your first and last statements or paragraphs strong and concise. People usually remember the first thing and the last thing they see or hear, so use that to your advantage. This helps your message stick in the receiver's mind. Effective communication always depends on a sender (the one with the message) and the receiver (the one receiving the message). Do everything you can to make the job easy for the receiver.

Ask questions to make sure your team heard what you were communicating. Miscommunications occur regularly because we assume people heard what we thought we were saying or writing. Solicit feedback

"Coaching" the Team

from team members and pay close attention to the non-verbal communication of team members. Be sensitive to what you think your team members are really trying to communicate to you.

Another aspect of coaching is to be positive and to help your team members be positive. This has to do with your attitude toward your life, not just your job. People who look for the best in a situation and who encourage others are usually like a ray of sunshine on a rainy day. You can keep that attitude by paying close attention to your self-talk. Self-talk is how we communicate with ourselves. It's the little voice in the back of our minds, and with most people it's a negative voice. Monitor the voice and change the messages from negative to positive. As Joe Gilliam regularly chants, "I'm alert, I'm alive, I feel great." Say that repeatedly to energize yourself.

When you are changing your message, keep three things in mind. The message needs to be in the present tense, first person and positive. An example would be, "I am having a wonderful day today." It's a matter of attitude, and you have a choice to make about your attitude. Make the choice to be positive about yourself and your job.

Also be positive toward your team members. Look for reasons to compliment them. Unfortunately for most of us, it's very easy to be negative about others and ourselves. Change that habit of negativity to a habit of being positive. When you are actively looking for the positive, you will find it much more easily. When you discover the positive in others, be sure to share it with them. Team members respond to compliments like flowers to a soft rain. Also remember to take this positive attitude home with you and let people in your personal life benefit from your new approach to life.

A coach has many roles and lots of tools to help fulfill these roles. The choice to be the coach of a successful team is yours. It will involve changing some habits, strengthening some skills, and being willing to take a risk, but the payoff is more than worth it. In order to continue building these skills, let's take a look at some of the characteristics of high-performance coaches.

COACHING

Characteristics of a High-Performance Coach

Tommy Lasorda said, "You've got to keep talking to your people. You've got to keep believing in them. You must be a confidence builder. I try to refrain from using the words 'can't,' 'won't,' 'I don't know,' 'maybe.' I want my men to say 'I can,' 'I will,' 'I must,' 'I shall,' 'I know.' You have to always try to do everything you can to help them maintain their confidence level. Put positive pictures in the minds of your staff. Your attitude is critical." This is a great description of a high-performance coach, so let's take a closer look at what Coach Lasorda feels is important.

Notice the first thing he mentions is, "You've got to keep talking to your people." Keeping the lines of communication open is critical to a team that functions effectively. We've already looked at some ways of communicating more effectively with team members. Another tool is to use open-ended questions effectively. Open-ended questions are questions that cannot be answered "yes" or "no." Because they're questions that cannot be answered with just one word, the questions will help you discover more about your team members.

Open-ended questions get the conversation moving and can create interaction between you and the team member. Practice writing out some open-ended questions to help you become comfortable using them. Instead of saying, "Are you okay today?" ask an open-ended question. "What's going on today?" gives the person an opportunity to start a dialogue with you and can give you insight into what the team member is thinking or feeling.

"You've got to keep believing in them" is another sign of an effective coach. This means that when a mistake is made the coach focuses on a solution, not on blame. This changes the entire emphasis for the team and encourages its creativity and ability to take a risk. Teams that are afraid of risk will often miss great opportunities for growth and new ways of solving problems.

Building confidence in the team is a primary tool that the coach has to help the team accomplish great things. This goes right along with believing in your team members, and this is vital if team members are to believe in themselves.

"Coaching" the Team

Building confidence means you'll be careful about the words you use when talking with the team.

Coach Lasorda says he avoids words that are negative and builds confidence by using positive words. Check out your communication pattern. How many positive words are you using? Does your communication pattern usually have a negative twist to it? Build confidence in your team so it will use powerful words like "I can," "I will," "I must," "I shall," "I know." In a book by Sam Horn called *Tongue Fu*, she has a list of words to use and words to lose. The first loser is "but."

"Put positive pictures in the minds of your staff. Your attitude is critical," Lasorda states. This is probably the heart of the matter, because you can have excellent communication skills and try to be a confidence builder and still not have an effective team because of your attitude. How do you maintain your positive attitude? Fill your mind with positive influences through the books you read, the tapes you listen to and the videos you watch. You can't give to others if you aren't building yourself.

Summary

In this chapter you've taken the time to look at how a leader can use the coach role with her team. We've also examined some of the reasons why coaching is so beneficial to a team. There are many reasons why leaders don't coach their teams, but coaching is necessary if the team is to be successful. The actions of a successful coach were examined along with the characteristics of a high-performance coach. When you use the tools in this chapter to build your own strengths as a person and as a coach, you are building for a successful tomorrow. Even with all these skills, the most important thing is still your own attitude. Having that positive outlook on your job and on life is necessary if you're going to coach, stretch, develop and encourage your team members.

Harvey S. Firestone said, "It is only as we develop others that we permanently succeed." Be a coach that permanently succeeds.

REFLECTIONS

What are you currently doing to maintain a positive attitude? List at least three things below:

1.

2.

3.

What will you start doing in the next 30 days to continue building a positive attitude, to be the type of coach who will help develop others? Write two ideas here:

1.

2.

Write the name of your favorite motivational speaker here. Who will benefit when you tell them about this motivational speaker? When will you tell them about your favorite speaker?

Motivational speaker: _____

I'll tell: _____

Date: _____

Reflections

5 "MENTORING" THE TEAM

We hear quite a bit today about mentoring. Schools are asking for mentors for elementary-, middle- and high-school students. Businesspeople are encouraged to mentor youth who are considered to be "at risk" of not becoming productive members of society. Some businesses have formal mentoring programs. Retired business professionals regularly mentor entrepreneurs. However, there are many different ideas about what it means to mentor someone. A mentor is someone who influences another person. We all influence other people, but the mentor influences another in order to help that person grow and develop. Countless successful businesses and organizations have formal mentoring programs to ensure executive development and succession.

Mentoring is the process of investing yourself in another person to help that person grow and improve. The mentor is the example, and the person being mentored begins to emulate the actions and abilities of the mentor, which produces growth and development. In this chapter we will examine some steps to mentoring, the benefits of mentoring and some roadblocks to mentoring. We'll also look at the actions and techniques of a mentor so you can build your mentoring skills. Leaders who are achievers look for people who want to grow and learn. Be alert for someone in whose life you can make a difference by serving as a mentor.

COACHING

What Does Mentoring Mean?

To mentor means to be a teacher or a coach, but it also carries the idea of spending time with the person who is mentored. Leaders who function as mentors are expected to stretch those involved in the mentoring process. This is a time-consuming process and requires patience on the part of the mentor as well as the team member being mentored. Be very careful about starting the mentoring process if you're not willing to take the time required. If you start and don't invest the time, you will make your team member feel like he is no longer valued or important to you or the team.

Jackie Robinson, the baseball great, said, "A life isn't significant except for its impact on others." It is when you, as a leader, move into the mentor role that you have the greatest opportunity to make an impact on other people. When you mentor a person, you can add tremendous value to his life.

— *Coach Joe Says ...*

By definition, mentoring is a relational experience whereby one person shares information with another. The mentor must be willing to invest his life in the life of the person being mentored.

The Benefits of Mentoring

One of the many benefits of mentoring is the opportunity for the person being mentored to be more proactive in career planning and job skills. As you encourage him to look at better ways of performing his job, you are helping him develop a teachable spirit. This is a wonderful gift because a person with a teachable spirit is always willing to learn something new. Not only is he willing, but he looks for opportunities to add to his knowledge and abilities. This willingness to be involved in lifelong learning brings about new insights and makes it easier to deal with change. When he thinks he knows all there is to know, he becomes stifled and dull and loses the competitive edge that fuels change and growth.

"Mentoring" the Team

Because he has a teachable spirit and is alert to new opportunities to learn, he is able to move toward being an expert in his field or an expert for his team. A mentor is able to point out areas that need to be strengthened in order for the person to become more proficient in handling job responsibilities. There is an orderly move toward becoming a specialist in his field. This knowledge can also make the person being mentored more promotable. As other departments or divisions recognize his skill level, the one being mentored becomes more valuable to the organization.

Another benefit of mentoring is helping the person become politically tuned in to what is happening in the organization. There are always power people who are not reflected on an organizational chart. There are things the organization does that aren't written in the handbook. When you mentor a person, you share knowledge about your corporate culture. You are serving as a guide within the organization. This helps the one being mentored develop sensitivity to the organizational culture so he can create a plan for working within that culture.

When you mentor someone, you introduce him to the power of networking. This means you help him create his own network of people he effectively relates to in other areas of the organization. Being able to cross department or division lines to get the job done depends on networking. This also helps him keep the big picture in mind because he's able to see things from different perspectives. He picks up these perspectives from the variety of people in his network.

One of the lasting benefits of mentoring is that it promotes more mentoring. When a person has been mentored, he is more likely to invest himself in the lives of other people. It is a process that continues to grow and influence long after your involvement in his life is over. Successful mentors see the potential in others and put them in a position to succeed.

COACHING

Why Leaders Should Mentor

Leaders should mentor because it is a way of helping other people grow and become more successful. When you invest in mentoring another person, you are creating a situation that will pay long-term benefits. The one being mentored becomes more skilled and confident as a result of your involvement in his life.

Mentoring will also free you up to do other tasks. Although mentoring takes time, it will also buy you time if you do it correctly. One effective way of mentoring is to delegate some of your tasks to the one being mentored. This shows you have confidence in the person and gives you the opportunity to help the person build his skills or abilities.

When you mentor, you benefit the team and the organization. The team benefits when members build their skills, because of the job proficiency that results. The one being mentored may build interpersonal skills that will help the team function more effectively and smoothly. The organization benefits when any of its employees improve their abilities and capabilities. The better skilled the team members are, the better their accomplishments will be. Also, when one or two team members improve their skills, the rest of the team members are pushed to strengthen their abilities and skills.

If you have a team that is consistently getting results that are less than what you desire, it is time for you to begin to function in the role of mentor. Take the time to identify the potential of team members, help them grow and be successful in one or more areas, and then watch the way your team benefits. When team members begin to expect success and satisfactory achievement, they have a more positive attitude, and your job as leader is easier.

Why Don't Leaders Mentor More?

Many leaders are reluctant to mentor their team members because they fear a loss of control. A leader may think, "If the team members know everything I know, they won't need me." What a false idea! When your team members know everything you know, you are free to move on up the organizational ladder.

"Mentoring" the Team

More than one leader has been stuck in their job because no one else could do it as well as they could. Don't let this happen to you — mentor your team members.

— Coach Joe Says ...

If you have been told you can't move to another position because "no one else knows how to do your job," this is a clear signal to you that mentoring is needed for your team members. Help them stretch and grow so you'll be able to also stretch and grow into another position.

Low self-esteem may be another reason a leader doesn't mentor his team members. If he doesn't feel competent or capable, he's not likely to try and teach team members anything. When he suffers from low self-esteem, he doesn't think he has any valuable knowledge or abilities to share with his team members. This attitude makes it difficult for him to share with anyone, whether or not they are on his team.

If the leader is a "know it all," the mentoring process will be foreign to his very existence. There are leaders who delight in keeping their team members in the dark. They dole out information like it was gold, and their teams are always struggling because members don't know what they need to know in order to do their jobs. This team leader becomes a bottleneck and creates unnecessary emergencies and problems because of his unwillingness to share information.

When Mentoring Is Most Beneficial

Mentoring is most beneficial when you have a team member who is eager to learn and willing to learn from the team leader.

COACHING

— *Coach Joe Says ...*

In order for a person to be mentored, they must have a teachable spirit. Spend your time and energy on people who have a desire to learn.

When you are mentoring people, look for someone who has a philosophy of life that is similar to yours. If you're going to invest your life in this person, it needs to be someone with similar values. Also, select people you really believe in, people you think really have potential. Invest yourself in people you believe will grow and make a difference with their lives.

Find people who can benefit from your knowledge or expertise. If people don't really need what you have to offer, don't invest in them. Use your strengths and experience to make a difference in the lives of people. Don't get involved in mentoring because you feel sorry for someone. That's a person you will need to counsel, nurture and motivate, but isn't a good candidate for mentoring.

Choose your time carefully. You need to be sensitive to the circumstances and situations in the other person's life. Just because it's convenient for you doesn't mean it is the best time for the other person. Mentoring needs to be purposeful and planned. It's a long, involved process, not something quickly and easily achieved.

Also, mentor the person for success. Not every person will be successful because they may limit themselves. They may not be willing to invest the time and energy needed to grow and expand. Don't try to push him beyond what he is willing to do. This can be very frustrating when you see someone with great potential but who lacks the drive or interest to really grow. Spend your time and energy on people who want to grow. If a person has the desire and isn't quite as talented, go with the one who has the desire. That drive and determination can produce miracles.

"Mentoring" the Team

Actions and Techniques of the Mentor

Mentors are able to see great potential in others. A mentor can help others discover and develop their potential. What interests another, what makes his face light up? Use your imagination to see what this person has the potential to achieve. Help motivate him to go for the future that the two of you envision. It's been said, "Don't let yourself be pressured into thinking that your dreams or your talents aren't prudent. They were never meant to be prudent. They were meant to bring joy and fulfillment into your life." Help him dream his wildest dreams and then see how those dreams can be fulfilled.

— *Coach Joe Says ...*

Dexter Yager says, "If the dream is big enough, the facts don't count."

Another task of the mentor is to find the passion that burns within that other person. Even the quietest people are passionate about something. What is it? When you find that passion, use the passion to help you motivate and inspire him. Help him to see that his dreams really can come true.

Of course, it is not enough just to point out that dreams can come true. Commitment and a willingness to grow and change are necessary before dreams can come true. You must help him build and use the abilities and strengths he has to accomplish these dreams. After you've established a good relationship with the person — when you are both comfortable working together — you can begin to deal with areas of weakness that need to be strengthened.

One other thing a mentor can do is to use conferences, seminars, articles, books or tapes to help him grow. Use any resources that will expand his knowledge base or information level. Share resources that you've found helpful. Remember the old saying, "Feed a man who is hungry today and he will be hungry again tomorrow. Teach him to fish and he will never be hungry again." Teach the ones you are mentoring "to fish" — show them where to go for additional information — and they will continue to grow in the days and years ahead.

COACHING

— *Coach Joe Says ...*

Mentoring hinges on the leader's desire to grow. If the leader isn't taking in new information, there will be no effective mentoring.

Smart Questions

The ability to ask smart questions makes it possible for you to gain information and insights to help you function more effectively as a mentor. Smart questions are the six questions that begin with five W's and an H.

- Who
- What
- When
- Where
- Why
- How

Learn to use these questions to help you have clarification and greater understanding of a situation.

— *Coach Joe Says ...*

Use "why" questions sparingly as they can invite defensiveness.

Practice using these questions until it is second nature for you to use them. You won't have to think about it anymore — they will come to you naturally.

The following are some examples of how you could use smart questions:

1. Why is this job important? If you are going to spend time helping him improve his job skills, you need to know why it's important.

"Mentoring" the Team

2. What are the key competencies of this job? When these are identified, you will know how to match the man to the job. Don't spend time trying to put square pegs in round holes.

3. What are the cautions? Identify any pitfalls that may come along with this job and make sure the one being mentored understands and is prepared to deal with them.

4. What timing issues are important? When you are mentoring, make sure there is enough time to allow for learning. Don't try to rush the learning process because that can cause failure, which leads to discouragement. That makes your job of mentoring even harder.

5. What's in this for me? Everyone has this as an underlying question. To mentor effectively, you need to be able to show how this knowledge or ability will benefit him. This provides the needed motivation to stick with the learning process even when the going gets rough. And we all know the going will get rough!

These questions were adapted from *The Manager's Role as Coach*, a National Seminars training manual. As you continue the mentoring process, you'll develop your own favorite questions to use in exploring the passions and interests of the one you're mentoring. By answering these questions for yourself, you will keep your approach fresh and new.

Since mentoring is a process, you'll need tools to help you be more effective, and questions should be part of your tool kit. You'll also need a plan for mentoring effectively. How will you participate in the life of the person you're mentoring? What boundaries will you set for the person? How will you conduct the mentoring process? These are additional questions you can use to help you perform the mentoring function.

COACHING

Summary

In this chapter we've looked more closely at the mentoring process. Since mentoring means both to instruct and lead by example, a wise leader builds skills so the team members also can grow and develop. The wise leader uses the mentoring process to help a team become more productive and effective. If the team isn't getting the desired results, the team leader can use the mentoring process to provide opportunities for team members' growth.

There are benefits to the team, the organization and the individual when effective mentoring occurs. Mentoring isn't easy or fast, but it pays great dividends. Eliminate the blocks to mentoring and use the techniques and tips outlined to help you be a more powerful mentor. Use smart questions to help you know more about the one being mentored. Build your skills as a mentor and make a difference in the lives of others.

When you are mentoring, don't forget to celebrate the victories. Mentoring is not designed to be all drudgery and no enjoyment, so take time to enjoy the successes. You'll be making an investment in the future. I can't think of a greater legacy than to have been the one who made a difference in the lives of other people, can you?

Jonathan Swift wrote, "Vision is the art of seeing things invisible." Mentoring enables vision to become reality in the lives of the people in whom you are willing to invest.

— *Coach Joe Says ...*

"Where there is no vision, the people perish."

REFLECTIONS

1. Think of one person you believe would benefit from being mentored. Write that person's name here.

2. Complete the following information for the person you named above:

    - What potential do you see in this person?

    - What is his passion?

    - What changes will he need to make to achieve his potential?

    - What books or tapes will you recommend to him as part of the mentoring process?

    - What seminars or training events would be beneficial to him?

3. When will you begin mentoring this person? Set a specific date, time and place for the first meeting to take place and write it here.

Reflections

Coaching

6 "COUNSELING" THE TEAM

Every leader sooner or later will find herself in the role of counselor with responsibility for confronting and correcting a team member who is functioning below performance standards. A leader will also be in the counselor role when helping team members deal with personal issues and problems that affect their work performance. There are three places to handle performance problems: at the front door during hiring, at the back door through termination, or in-house through counseling.

What Is a Counselor?

When you are functioning as a counselor, you are not attempting to provide psychological therapy. Instead, you are using your best interpersonal skills to help resolve people problems that your team members may have. The objective in counseling is to make clear the effect of continued poor performance on the team's effort. You must also communicate the need for an immediate change in behavior. In counseling your team member, the goal is to identify the cause of the problem behavior, change the behavior for the benefit of the team, and sometimes even make a decision about the member's continued presence on the team.

An effective counselor will lead the team member to accept more responsibility after identifying strategies for improved performance. You will need to lead the team member to commit to improve her performance and also allow an opportunity for her to vent strong feelings or emotions. You'll be in a position to help the team member overcome obstacles and fears that may be interfering with her performance as a team member.

When to Counsel

As Ferdinand Fournies points out in his book *Why Employees Don't Do What They're Supposed to Do*, many team members don't perform effectively because they don't know how. (See Table, Appendix B, page 105.) He feels that as many as 80 percent of the people who are identified as failing are failing because they haven't been taught how to do the job. It's not that they won't perform the job, it's that they've never been taught how to perform the job. You have the opportunity to coach these team members so they can be more successful on the team and in the workplace. (Also, review "Why People Don't Do What They Are Supposed to Do," in chapter 3.)

When you have team members who need their job skills strengthened, you will identify job training that is needed, the best way to deliver that training, and see that it takes place. That may mean working alongside a team member as the skills are built. However, it's also effective to pair that team member with another person who has the job skills that are needing to be developed. This allows you to encourage and support and, at the same time, help build self-esteem and confidence of both team members. Peer training can also help build team spirit because people are generally more supportive of someone they've helped. Delegating is as effective in coaching as it is for general management.

The Benefits of a Counselor Role

One of the benefits of functioning in the counseling role is your ability to influence team members and help them be enthusiastic about the task that needs to be done. The counseling leader makes sure everyone knows their responsibilities and boundaries. There are few, if any, surprises for the leader who is effective as a counselor, because this leader is alert to what is happening with team members.

"Counseling" the Team

The leader who acts as a counselor helps resolve people problems and then attempts to prevent these types of problems from happening again. If it is a serious personal issue such as finances or an ongoing conflict with a family member, the leader/counselor can't solve the problem. She can encourage the team member to take advantage of a trained counselor who is skilled in the particular problem area. Point the team member in the direction of an expert in the field.

If the problem is work-related, such as priorities shifting or a team member being overwhelmed with work, the leader/counselor helps solve the immediate problem. Then she attempts to prevent this type of problem from recurring. This may mean a change in team procedures or a realignment of the team member's tasks or any of a dozen different actions. These actions are usually directed at the team member rather than the whole team.

Counseling can help with generational clashes. The 50-something employees have trouble respecting the 20-something employees. They don't think they have a work ethic. The 20-somethings don't respect the 50-somethings. They think they have no life after work, no sense of balance or priorities. Counseling can greatly help in this negative situation.

Why Leaders Don't Counsel

Counseling can be difficult to do because it requires a confrontation. Most people will avoid confrontation rather than deal with the negative feelings it usually generates. When you confront the person, remember to be honest, take the initiative, time the confrontation well, mean what you say and be human. Some people avoid confrontation because they are afraid they'll be rejected or disliked. We occasionally think that if we wait long enough, the situation will get better all by itself! Or we may think we'll make the situation worse if the person is confronted with her inappropriate behavior.

Actually, when you confront someone, you're really letting her know how much you value her as a person and as a member of the team. If you don't confront the person, you're allowing her to cause you to fail. When your team member isn't functioning effectively, it reflects negatively on you as a leader. It also is a negative influence for the other team members. It makes their task harder, and they may feel unappreciated and undervalued. It also causes the whole organization to suffer because the team isn't able to deliver its best effort or result.

When you confront a person, you are offering her an opportunity for learning and growth. Think of this confrontation as a chance to develop the person, as an opportunity to build her performance skills or her interpersonal skills. As difficult as confrontation is, you must remember that any behavior not confronted will continue. The situation will not take care of itself, so you must move into the counselor role for the benefit of the team, yourself and the organization.

Confrontation

Confrontation is usually not a favorite activity of any leader; however, there are some things you can do to make the confrontation more effective. When you're involved in confrontation, remember to confront the behavior, not the person. These are some questions you need to ask yourself before you begin the confrontation process.

1. Is this the best time for the confrontation? When you are angry or upset is usually not the best time for a confrontation. You also want to choose a time when the other person is calm rather than trying to deal with the situation if the person is frustrated or too busy to listen effectively.

2. Is this the best way to communicate with this person? In most cases you need to meet face to face with the individual so you can read her body language and other non-verbal signals. This also allows the other person to read your non-verbal signals, and that can help her understand how important this issue is to you.

3. Is this the best place for a confrontation? Confrontations should be in private, preferably in a room with a door that can be closed for privacy.

"Counseling" the Team

4. Is this the best person to confront? A leader may occasionally confront the one that's being mentored simply because of the relationship that has been established. Always ask yourself why this person needs to be involved in this confrontation. Maybe she isn't the one who needs to hear it after all.

Use the Burger Technique explained in Chapter Two and focus on what can be changed. When you confront the team member, always bring at least one suggestion for improvement. Don't confront without having something positive to contribute. Be specific in the behavior you are dealing with and ask for feedback from the one being confronted. Be sincere in asking for feedback because this can be an opportunity for you to learn more about this team member. After dealing with the solution you and the team member have agreed upon, be sure to reaffirm her value and worth to the team, to you personally and to the organization. This gives you an opportunity to let her know you still value her, even though she made a mistake. Again, remember to confront mistakes or behaviors, but don't attack the individual.

Additional techniques for confronting include phrases such as:

- I'm puzzled. How is it that ...?
- I'm uncomfortable with this
- Help me understand ...

John Wooden said, "If you're not making mistakes, then you're not doing anything. I'm positive that a doer makes mistakes." Wooden knew about working with teams because he was the outstanding basketball coach for UCLA for years and led them to seven successive national titles. Look at your team and see what kinds of mistakes team members are making. Use that information as part of your counseling process to build skills to overcome areas in which the team is deficient. Ask the person being counseled for her input about the situation, and then together come up with a solution that is agreed on by both of you.

COACHING

How to Use the Counseling Role Effectively

When one or more team members aren't performing as they should, use performance standards to outline the results you expect from each team member. Make sure every member of the team understands and accepts these standards. It can be effective to have the team help establish the standards so there is agreement with the standards as well as buy-in from team members. People generally find it easier to support something they helped generate.

Performance standards need to be specific so everyone knows exactly what is expected of them. They also need to be measurable. If you can't validate the standard, how will you know when it is being achieved? To be effective, standards also need to be realistic. Performance standards can be discouraging if they seem impossible to accomplish. When team members are discouraged about the standards, they will resist them and, in some cases, even actively work against the standards imposed on the team.

The leader will also use the counselor role to help a team member deal with personal matters that affect the work of the member and the team. If you have established a good working relationship with your team members, the role of counselor will be easier for you to fill. Team members will feel comfortable with you because a trust level has been built, and the members know that anything shared with you will be kept confidential. If you usually show an interest in team members, it won't seem unusual when you show an interest in what is happening in their lives.

When you are counseling your team member, start by making sure she knows what is acceptable performance. Ask about a current project or task she is responsible for or in which she is deeply involved. If there seems to be difficulty in completing the project, ask for information from your team member by using some open-ended questions. What areas of this project are giving you trouble? What outside influences are causing you trouble? Some well-thought-out, open-ended questions give the team member an opportunity to share personal information with you.

You must be willing to invest time in the person because she may be hesitant to share any personal information with you at first. You might have to

"COUNSELING" THE TEAM

meet with her a second time before she trusts you enough to open up and share what's really bothering her. Your purpose is to support and encourage the team member. You're not there to provide in-depth psychological counseling, but everyone benefits from a sympathetic ear once in a while. Be willing to support your team members by spending time with them one-on-one, so they can build the trust and confidence that is important for you to be able to function in the counseling role.

Actions of a "Counselor"

Counseling your team member is a six-step process. The first step is to describe the situation. This means you have gathered your facts, and you are dealing with reality, not innuendo and suspicions. Don't be judgmental toward the team member, but point out to her that the situation needs to be handled quickly because the behavior is interfering with the successful performance of the team. This situation or behavior is also preventing the team member from giving her best effort to the team, so she isn't living up to her potential as a person or as a team member. Remind her that when any team member isn't performing at an acceptable level, the whole team suffers.

— *Coach Joe Says ...*
When a team isn't reaching its full potential, it isn't getting results.

Then listen to what the team member has to say. Let her explain what is happening. This is the time to use your active listening skills. Lean forward, show interest in what she's saying, nod your head, and paraphrase back what you've heard. Don't interrupt or try to justify or defend your position, performance standards, team tasks or the behavior of other team members. This is about the behavior or lack of performance of this one team member, so stay focused on the real issue and what you want to accomplish in this counseling role. Most people will believe you really want to help them if you listen carefully to what they have to say. This makes it easier for you to move to the next step of counseling.

Coaching

When the team member has finished her explanation, then you need to restate the behavior and the consequences of continuing that behavior. Encourage her to accept responsibility for her behavior by first defining what it means to be responsible, and then by focusing on the facts. You need to be sure the team member is very clear about what will occur if her behavior does not change. It is important that the team member realize this behavior is not acceptable and won't be tolerated because of the negative impact it has on the team. There is nothing personal here if you stay focused on the team's objectives and tasks.

When you are counseling a team member, the two of you need to work together to come up with an action plan that will correct the situation. Explore problem-solving options together. The solution may be as simple as helping the team member realign some of her job priorities. You might have to reassign some of her responsibilities so she is using her strengths. When the team assignments were first given, her strengths may not have been well known, so look for options that will help her be successful.

Remember your goal is to help every member of the team be successful. This takes time because we don't always know the best person for the task, especially when a team is first forming. If the solution to the problem is suggested by the person being counseled, or she has a part in deciding the solution, she is more likely to follow through with the agreement. Taking the time to reach a common agreement pays off in great benefits for the one being counseled because it builds her sense of control and accomplishment. It pays off for you as a leader because you have salvaged a team member and helped your team perform more effectively. You must get a commitment for action because this is when the team member accepts responsibility for changing her behavior. There must be a concrete action plan before you are ready for the last step in the counseling process.

The last step is to provide feedback and support as the change takes place. This may mean regular meetings to encourage and affirm the actions that are taking place. It might mean a note or e-mail to give support. It might be an affirmation during a team meeting when she makes a contribution that is a result of improvement in her behavior. It might be a deadline kept, a report

"Counseling" the Team

that was completed, or help given to another team member. Be alert to ways of supporting her as the behavior changes. In whatever manner you follow up, you must check the team member's progress regularly. This allows you to deal with any problems quickly and shows the team member you're interested in her success.

Good feedback is constructive feedback and highlights how the team member is doing. It points out areas that could be strengthened or how the team member could do better next time. This means you, as the leader-counselor, need to be sensitive. Be sure to focus on observable, specific facts, not on the traits of the person. Acknowledge the feelings of your team member, but focus on building or improving the behavior. Ask her to tell you how she sees her progress or improvement. Let her assess her own performance. This can provide a starting place for the feedback session.

When you are counseling, you must be patient. People are different. They have different abilities, skills and interests. Be patient with the differences and allow your team members to develop skills and gain experience at their own rate or level. Because people are different, you need to be flexible in your approach. Recognize the differences and use that diversity to strengthen your team rather than try to make every team member fit one mold.

A Word of Caution

Don't attempt to give advice about serious personal issues. As a leader you are to support, encourage, develop and build up your team members. You are not to function as a psychologist. Listen to the team member carefully and help her put the problem in perspective. Sometimes just hearing you rephrase the situation will help her decide what needs to be done. You can suggest outside resources to help her deal with the problem area. This may include professional counseling, but you must be careful how you phrase this to your team member. Remind her that seeking professional counseling is no different than going to the doctor when your leg is broken. We think nothing about seeking medical help for physical ailments, yet hesitate to even consider psychological help when we are broken in spirit.

COACHING

Many companies have an employee assistance program that uses professional counselors who are trained to deal with specific issues. Everything that happens between the professional counselor and your team member is confidential. You'll never know what is discussed in their time together. You will be able to see the results in a team member who is happier, functioning effectively, and filling her role on the team. Sometimes the best help you can give the team member is a referral to more competent counseling.

— *Coach Joe Says ...*

This may also be a good time to refer her to a book or tape that you have found to be helpful.

Whatever decision your team member makes, let her know you are supportive of her. As difficult as it is, you can't judge, moralize or withdraw as a result of what the person has shared with you. If she trusted you enough to confide in you, you're responsible for helping find a solution so the team member can continue to be a part of the team. Your goal is to salvage this team member and help her be productive for the team, for you and for the organization.

Checking Out Your Counseling Skills

Here are some statements you can use to evaluate your effectiveness as a leader who counsels your team members. These are from the book *The High-value Manager,* by Florence M. Stone and Randi T. Sachs.

1. When a team member lets the team down, I remain objective about the member being counseled.

2. I make clear to team members what is expected of them both individually and as a part of the team.

3. I help members have access to the information and people they need to do their team assignments.

"Counseling" the Team

4. I share decision making with the team members.

5. I let those responsible for some part of the team effort decide for themselves how the job will be done.

6. I have identified within the team those informal leaders who can help me coach and counsel the other members.

7. I make sure that everyone on the team knows who "owns" what assignments.

8. I intervene when an attitude problem or other situation is counterproductive to the team's mission.

9. I keep team members informed of developments that might call for a shift in mission or effort.

10. I monitor the team effort to see that it is meeting its schedule and is on track.

11. I anticipate problems and act to prevent them from occurring.

If you are able to answer "always" or "almost always" to each of these questions, you're doing an awesome job of counseling your team members when they need it. If you weren't able to answer "always" or "almost always," use these questions to help you know where to concentrate on building your skills as a leader who is effective as a counselor.

Remember to model what you are constantly teaching your team members. Since professional growth is part of what you teach, it needs to be part of what you model for them. Leadership skills are "caught" as much as they are "taught!"

COACHING

Summary

In the counseling role you, as a leader, are helping individual team members deal with issues and problems that are interfering with their job performance. It may be a lack of understanding exactly what is expected of them, so you provide performance standards. It might be something in a team member's personal life that is interfering with her ability to function as an effective member of the team. That is when you use your best listening skills and encourage her to take care of the issues, even if this requires professional counseling. Be aware that counseling requires confrontation. The leader who learns to counsel her team effectively is building a strong foundation for her work area. This reflects positively on her because she has continued to help her people develop even in difficult circumstances.

"The most pathetic person in the world is someone who has sight but has no vision." This statement by Helen Keller is a powerful reminder that people need to have a vision, a goal that drives, inspires and motivates them to achieve greater results than they ever expected. Counsel your team member when anything interferes with her achieving her vision.

REFLECTIONS

1. Think of someone you could offer some constructive feedback to today.

2. What would you like to say to this person that would be positive? Write out a suggested opening for a feedback session with this person.

3. What would be the body of your message to this team member? What would you want to have happen as a result of your time together?

4. How would you follow up with this person? Write down at least two actions you could take to follow up.

    a.

    b.

5. Set two dates for formal follow-up sessions.

    a.

    b.

Reflections

Coaching

7 DEVELOPING HABITS FOR HIGH PERFORMANCE

Coach Bear Bryant, the legendary football coach at Alabama, said, "I'm just a plowhand from Arkansas, but I have learned how to hold a team together — how to lift some men up, how to calm others down, until finally they've got one heartbeat together as a team. There are always just three things I say: 'If anything goes bad, I did it. If anything goes semi-good, then we did it. If anything goes real good, they did it.' That's all it takes to get people to win."

High-performance coaches are people who have learned how to hold a team together. Coach Bryant states so simply and yet so completely what is required to be a high-performance coach. This is a person who has learned how to bring out the very best in others. He has developed his people skills so he knows which team members need to be lifted up and which ones need to be calmed down. The high-performance coach invests himself in other people. This is the coach who knows how to work with the team until it has one heartbeat, one vision, one dream!

The high-performance coach is one who has a vision for the team and is able to make that vision come alive. He can see the big picture, but inspires and motivates his team members by helping them see how they help fulfill the vision. He builds a sense in them that they are vital to accomplishing the vision. This is a coach who believes very strongly in the value of every player on the team. The high-performance coach isn't afraid of developing people, because he thinks the highest goal is to help someone else grow enough to take his job or even a better one! This coach knows he can't take his team where he isn't willing to go himself, so he invests in personal growth.

COACHING

Personal Growth

Alan Loy McGinnis, author, wrote, "There is no more noble occupation in the world than to assist another human being — to help someone succeed." You can't do this unless you are constantly learning and growing. When you have the goal to continually learn, you won't be a person who can be used up. You'll always be recharging your batteries, gaining new ideas and insights, and finding new ways to do things.

High-performance coaches know that the "way we've always done things" is now a thing of the past. The old management style of telling people what to do and then watching to see that they do it right is long gone. The norms are gone; the stakes are changing at an exponential rate. That means high-performance coaches are constantly in a state of learning and growing. Because you desire to be a high-performance coach, one who makes a difference in the lives of others, you will be constantly growing and learning also.

You will build your planning skills. There is a vast array of new technology that you can use to help with your planning. There are project management software packages that stay on top of projects with less time needed from you. There are personal digital assistants that keep vast amounts of information at your fingertips. Memos, calendars, expenses, thoughts and ideas can all be carried in your shirt pocket or purse. Take advantage of technology and spend time learning to use it in order to have more time for your people. Don't burden yourself with gadgets you don't need — focus on what will aid you.

Seminars, workshops, personal and professional growth training experiences can also help you maintain your role as a high-performance coach. It's easy to forget some of the basics, so take the time to move out of your own little corner of the world. Expand your horizons with outside training. Network with people outside your organization and even outside your industry. This helps you expand your horizons. Use on-line learning and one-on-one development efforts as much for yourself as for your team.

DEVELOPING HABITS FOR HIGH PERFORMANCE

Build your relationship skills because you will never become too skilled at working with people. Monitor your communication skills. Are you talking more than you're listening? Listening is a powerful tool for the high-performance coach. Don't become so enthralled with the information and knowledge you have to share that you forget to listen to your team members. They also have great insights and perspectives that you don't have.

Herman Cain, in his book *Leadership is Common Sense*, writes, "When you dream again, you are able to recognize that problems are merely dangerous opportunities that could unlock the doors to your success." High-performance coaches don't run from problems but see them as opportunities. This leader is proactive and doesn't sit around waiting for things to happen — he makes things happen! Build your problem-solving skills and continue building them so your team will continue to be a high-performance team.

The high-performance coach knows that teaching, learning, building relationships and influencing people are the ingredients needed for a good leader. He keeps going back to the basics and building on those in his own personal life. Because of that he is ready to make a difference in the lives of his team members.

Moving In and Out of One's Comfort Zone

It is difficult to move out of our comfort zone. Most of us have worked hard to get where we are and we value the comfort zone. We forget that where we are now was not always comfortable. We had to learn how to be comfortable here. That means we can also learn how to be comfortable when we've done a little more stretching and growing. We must move out of our comfort zone. In order to do that, use the four "P's" so the move will be as easy as possible.

The first "P" is for planning. All high-performance coaches excel at planning. Things don't happen by accident but by design in a team that has a high-performance coach. When there is a plan that everyone knows about, it gives your people the ability to move forward without your constant attention.

They know how to set priorities, assign resources and keep working until they get the job done. A well-publicized plan makes the difference. Plan for your individual team players.

It's not enough for you as a high-performance coach to be skilled at planning. You also need to be practicing your plan, the second "P". You need to be practicing your people skills, and your use of open-ended questions and active listening to help your team become a high-performance team. Practice with your team players.

The third "P" is for patience. When you are working with people, you need to be patient. Expect people to be resistant to any changes you want the team to make and any new way of doing their tasks. Resistance is a natural reaction to anything new, and you must be patient with your people as they work through this reaction. Use patience with your team players.

Persisting is the fourth "P" in the formula. When you are mentoring team members, you'll need to be persistent in encouraging them and stretching them. When you are counseling a team member, you'll need to be persistent in your follow-up and feedback. When coaching your team, you'll have to be persistent in keeping them focused on the tasks and objectives. Persisting is one of the keys to becoming a high-performance coach. You can't afford to give up too soon, and that's what many leaders do — they just quit too soon! Persist with your team players.

Your role is to develop people. This is your opportunity to encourage your team members, challenge them, inspire them, excite them; in other words, make a difference in their lives. In order to do this, you must move out of your comfort zone. You won't make much of a difference if you aren't willing to be different!

High-Performance Skills

The high-performance coach knows the importance of setting goals. He sets goals for himself and makes sure these are SMART goals. SMART goals have the following five aspects:

DEVELOPING HABITS FOR HIGH PERFORMANCE

1. Specific — goals need to be definite and have a defined objective

2. Measurable — goals allow you to measure progress and to know when they have been achieved

3. Action — goals include the steps needed to achieve them, a plan of action

4. Realistic — goals should stretch you and your team members, but should also be seen as achievable

5. Time frame — goals need time limits in order to be valuable

The high-performance coach knows that he needs to lead his team to set goals and establish performance standards. He shares his knowledge and skills with his team members so they can also be successful.

This leader expects the very best from himself. He is willing to pay the price by making a commitment, setting goals and then staying with the plan. He knows the time will come when it'll be easier to abandon his goals, take the easy path and settle for less. That's when the commitment to be the very best helps him stay on track.

This leader not only believes he is empowered, but he is willing to empower his team members. This is a person who encourages other people, gives them recognition, and provides them with a sense of worth in their jobs. He is able to do this because he feels empowered as a high-performance coach. He keeps the team focused on its objectives so it will be successful. He does that not only to get the job done, but also because he knows this will keep the team motivated and functioning for maximum achievement.

This leader inspires and motivates people. He believes in developing others and helping others build their strengths. He spends time planning and preparing how he can best develop his team members. He communicates effectively and passionately about personal and professional development. He is enthusiastic about the organization he works for and sees himself as an integral part of its success.

COACHING

The high-performance coach believes in the people who work with him. He knows they have strengths and he creates an environment where they can utilize those strengths. When team assignments are given, he makes sure each team member is set up for success. He also knows that team members have weaknesses and he helps the team compensate for them. Because he believes in his team members, he is willing to invest in mentoring the ones who have a desire to learn and grow.

He creates a desire to excel by unlocking the passion each member of the team has lurking somewhere within them. He spends time helping team members become aware of their passions, and then channeling those passions so the team becomes a high-performance team. With this leader, it's not business as usual. It's business unusual! He constantly challenges his team members in order to bring out the best in them.

He also builds such an atmosphere of trust and openness that those team members feel secure in taking risks and making decisions. They're able to do that because they clearly understand the goals and philosophy of the organization. This frees them to exercise initiative and creativity while still maintaining a team that is focused on what needs to be done.

This coach knows how to ask the right questions. He asks questions that bring about clarification, inspire a new way of looking at things, or make the situation clearer. The right questions help keep the team focused. Work on your ability to ask questions — the right questions. When you ask the right questions, your team is able to make more right decisions.

Making right decisions creates a winning team, and nothing builds morale and enthusiasm faster than being a winner. You need to help your team be a winning team and then make sure it gets the recognition a winning team deserves. We all like to win. We like it even better when someone else notices we are winning.

Developing Habits for High Performance

Character of a High-Performance Coach

Even though these things have been mentioned in previous chapters, I believe they need to be said again. There are some absolutes that the high-performance coach needs to remember. One is the importance of integrity in the leader. When you have integrity, you'll commit yourself to people over things, to principle over convenience, and to character over personal gain. The great value of having integrity is that people never have to wonder where they stand with you. Integrity builds trust. When people trust you, they don't have to worry about what you have in mind. They know what your motives are, and those motives will be to benefit the team and the organization. They will know because you are consistent, a person of integrity.

This does not mean that you are harsh or uncaring, because a high-performance coach is one who nurtures people. You do need to let people know they are valuable to you, the team and the organization. Respect and recognition are two ways of letting a person know he is valued. When you respect him, you'll acknowledge his ability and potential to contribute. You'll treat him well and let him know that his feelings are important, his opinions are valuable and his preferences are respected.

You will also give your team members recognition whenever you can. This motivates your team members and builds them up. William A. Ward wrote, "Flatter me, and I may not believe you. Criticize me, and I may not like you. Ignore me, and I may not forgive you. Encourage me, and I will not forget you." To be unforgettable to your team members, encourage them and give them recognition.

Summary

To be a high-performance coach requires many different skills, and we've examined some of them in this chapter. However, you can have goals, make commitments, develop habits and do many other things to be a high-performance coach and still not be successful. It takes three qualities to build that success, and you can remember them by thinking of the three "D's" for success.

COACHING

The first "D" is for desire. You must have the desire to grow, excel and be a high-performance coach. I'm confident you have that desire, or you wouldn't be reading this. It is desire that prompted you to see what's available that will help you build your leadership skills

However, desire isn't enough. It must be accompanied by dedication. It will require dedication to complete the reflections in the book and then follow through with some of the decisions you've made. Dedication is what motivates you to begin to practice a new way of working with your team members. Dedication is what drives you to continue to build your skills as a leader.

But there are three "D's" because desire and dedication won't do it without discipline. Discipline is why you keep trying even when you don't feel comfortable. When the new way of leading doesn't seem to be working, discipline makes it possible for you to still try it one more time.

Teddy Roosevelt said, "The best executive is the one who has sense enough to pick good men to do what he wants done, and self-restraint enough to keep from meddling with them while they do it." I'd like to paraphrase that to read, "The best leader is the one who has sense enough to develop the best people to get done what should be done, and self-restraint enough to keep from meddling with them while they do it." Lead, develop, let members know what should be done, and then step back while your team moves to greater heights than they ever thought possible!

REFLECTIONS

Look at the habits of a high-performance coach. Which one of these habits do you want to strengthen? Write the habit down here:

What specific steps will you need to take to build that habit? Use SMART goals to help you with your action plan.

Specific:

Measurable:

Action:

Realistic:

Time frame:

Review this every day to help you stay focused on the goal you have set for yourself as you become even more powerful as a high-performance coach.

Reflections

Coaching

APPENDIX A

SELF — A Profile of Interpersonal Interactions

Each of us is unique. We all have different perceptions, values and experiences that make us special. The SELF Profile is a survey of social style dimensions that is designed to:

- Identify your particular style, that is, how you relate most often.
- Help you to gain a better understanding of yourself and others.
- Help you predict how you and others might respond in a given situation.
- Improve your communication with others that have different styles, therefore, building more meaningful relationships.

The SELF Profile has four distinct social styles of interaction with others. Although all of us are a unique blend of all four styles, you will be able to identify your dominant style. SELF was developed by using the most sophisticated techniques available, but it cannot provide accurate feedback if you do not provide accurate responses. Therefore, it is best to answer the questions in the way that you behave now rather than the way you used to be or would most like to be. Remember, no personality style is better than any other. And, honest answers will provide you with the most accurate, useful information possible.

SELF Directions:

The SELF Profile consists of 30 general questions describing how a person might act in a given situation.

How to Coach an Effective Team

- For questions 1-24, use the 1-5 scale listed in the example below describing how you might act in a given situation.
- For questions 25-30, choose A or B whichever response describes you best.

    Example: I consider myself to be good at small talk.

1	2	3	4	5
Not at all like me	Somewhat like me	Occasionally like me	Usually like me	Very much like me

Guidelines for Using This Information

When you have completed the SELF Profile and have access to more information for understanding others, there are a few guidelines that may be useful to remember.

- First, the information in this test is designed to aid you in self-awareness and understanding others in broad and general terms. However, there will be, as is always the case, exceptions to these general categories. Human beings are very complex creatures whose behavior is greatly affected by a variety of factors. Therefore, they are not easily categorized.

- Second, always remember that an individual's behavior is greatly affected by the situation s/he is in. So, you can expect individuals to exhibit a variety of different characteristics in different situations. Therefore, look for consistent information across several settings before categorizing others into any one dimension.

- Finally, it will help you to remember that an individual's social style is the product of many years of development and is not easily changed. You will be wise to accept others as they are — for both their strengths and limitations — rather than insisting upon changing them.

- Remember, no personality style is better than any other. Yet, our social interactions with others can be greatly enhanced if we have an understanding of the motivations, strengths and weaknesses of both ourselves and others. The SELF Profile can serve as a useful tool for gathering such information.

Excerpted from National Press Publications, Inc. SELF PROFILE, a division of National Seminars Group
© Copyright 1988 National Press Publications, Inc.

APPENDIX A

Please place the number that describes you best in the boxes on page 99.

1	2	3	4	5
Not at all like me	Somewhat like me	Occasionally like me	Usually like me	Very much like me

1. When in a group, I tend to speak and act as the representative of that group.
2. I am seldom quiet when I am with other people.
3. When faced with a leadership position, I tend to actively accept that role rather than diffuse it among others.
4. I would rather meet new people than read a good book.
5. Sometimes I ask more from my friends or family than they can accomplish.
6. I enjoy going out frequently.
7. It's important to me that people follow the advice that I give them.
8. I like to entertain guests.
9. When I am in charge of a situation, I am comfortable assigning others to specific tasks.
10. I often go out of my way to meet new people.
11. In social settings, I find myself asking more questions of others than they ask of me.
12. I often find myself playing the role of leader and taking charge of the situation.
13. I truly enjoy mixing in a crowd.
14. When I see that things aren't going smoothly in a group, I usually take the lead and try to bring some structure to the situation.
15. I make friends very easily.
16. Other people usually think of me as being energetic.
17. I am a verbal person.
18. I try to be supportive of my friends, no matter what they do.
19. I seldom find it hard to really enjoy myself at a lively party.
20. When in a leadership position, I like to clearly define my role and let followers know what is expected.
21. I consider myself to be good at small talk.
22. I am very good at persuading others to see things my way.
23. I can usually let myself go and have fun with friends.
24. I do not prefer the simple, quiet life.

HOW TO COACH AN EFFECTIVE TEAM

Notes

APPENDIX A

For questions 25-30 please write in the letter representing your response in the boxes on page 99.

25. You are in a conversation with more than one person. Someone makes a statement that you know is incorrect but you are sure the others didn't catch it. Do you let them know?
    A. Yes
    B. No
26. After a hard day's work I prefer to:
    A. Get together with a few friends and do something active.
    B. Relax at home and either watch TV or read.
27. When planning a social outing with a small group, I am most likely to:
    A. Be the first to suggest some plans and try to get the others to make a decision quickly.
    B. Make sure everyone has a say in the planning and go along with what the group decides.
28. You have just finished a three-month project for which you have sacrificed a great deal of your free time and energy. To celebrate, are you more likely to:
    A. Invite some of your friends over and throw a party.
    B. Spend a quiet, peaceful weekend doing whatever you wish, either by yourself or with a special friend.
29. If I feel that I am underpaid for my work, I'm most likely to:
    A. Confront the boss and demand a raise.
    B. Do nothing and hope the situation improves.
30. I think that those around me see me as primarily:
    A. Gregarious and outgoing.
    B. Introspective and thoughtful.

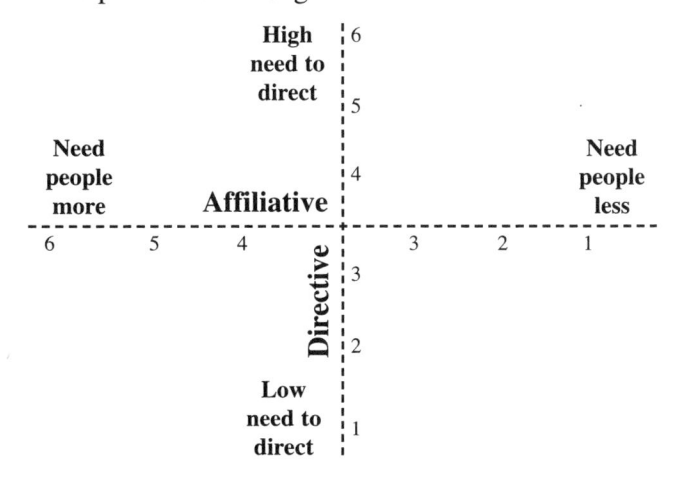

HOW TO COACH AN EFFECTIVE TEAM

Notes

APPENDIX A

To Score Your SELF Profile:
1. On items 25-30:
   - If you answered A, give yourself a 5.
   - If you answered B, give yourself a 1.
2. Now transfer each of the scores you've entered on the right to the blanks below.
3. Add each column.

1.	_____	2.	_____
3.	_____	4.	_____
5.	_____	6.	_____
7.	_____	8.	_____
9.	_____	10.	_____
11.	_____	12.	_____
13.	_____	14.	_____
15.	_____	16.	_____
17.	_____	18.	_____
19.	_____	20.	_____
21.	_____	22.	_____
23.	_____	24.	_____
25.	_____	26.	_____
27.	_____	28.	_____
29.	_____	30.	_____

Total _____   Total _____

DIRECTIVE SCORE _____   **AFFILIATIVE SCORE** _____

If you scored from:	Give yourself a:
15 – 21	1
22 – 33	2
34 – 44	3
45 – 56	4
57 – 68	5
69 – 75	6

- Take your Directive Score and put a dot on the broken line. The Directive Line shows an individual's needs and tendencies to direct and control situations. People scoring high on this line tend to be comfortable supervising others and controlling situations, while those scoring low on this line are generally more supportive and seek consensus from others.
- Then put a dot on the dotted line for your Affiliative Score. The Affiliative Line measures your needs and desires for being around others. If you scored high on the line, you probably like it best when you're with people. On the other hand, people with low scores on this line tend to be more self-contained, enjoy time to themselves or with a few close friends, and generally seek less interaction with others.
- Next, connect the two dots with a straight line.
- Shade in the area between the line you've drawn and the intersection of the broken and dotted lines.

How to Coach an Effective Team

SELF Characteristics

Below are some characteristics that can be used to describe the tendencies of each dimension of SELF.

STRENGTHS

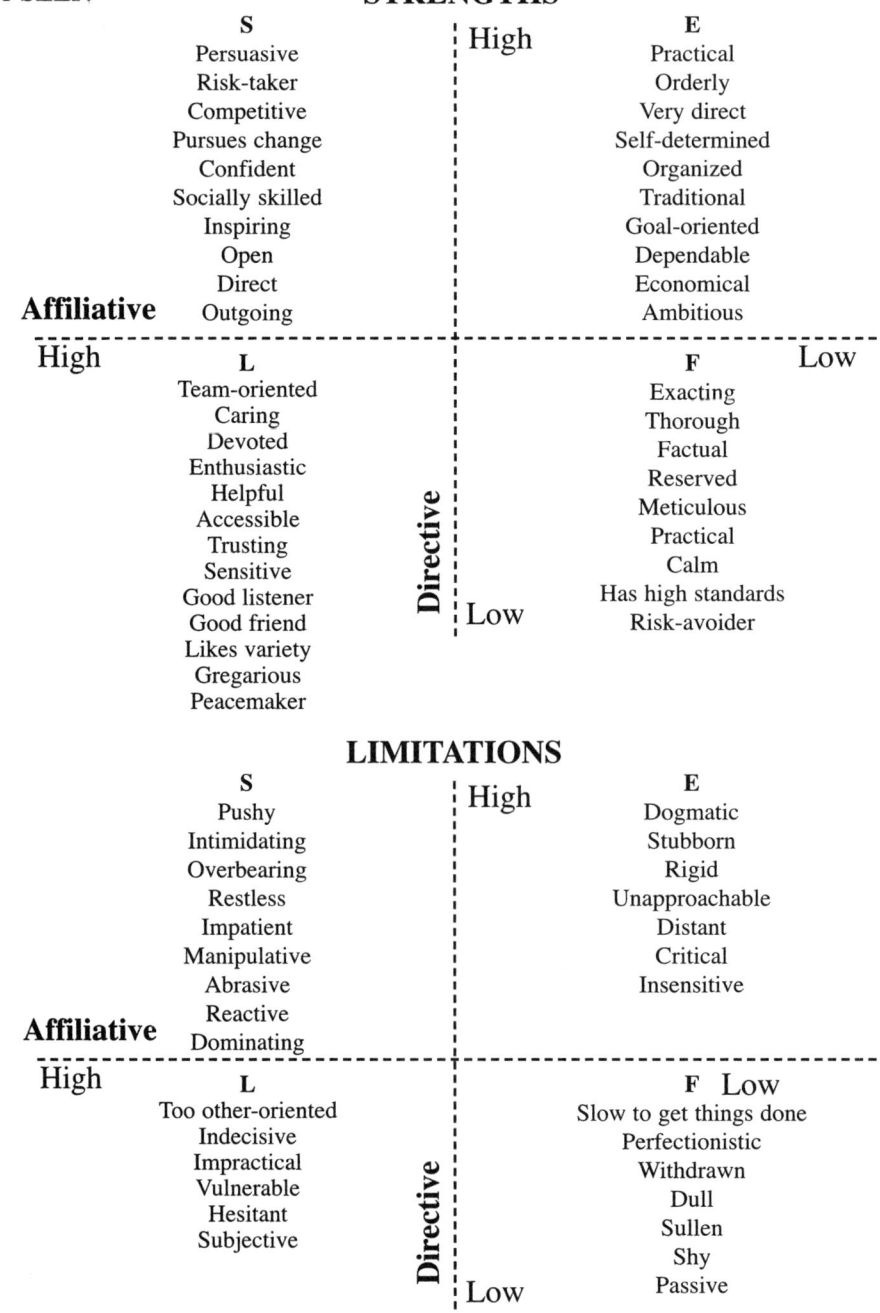

	S High	E
	Persuasive	Practical
	Risk-taker	Orderly
	Competitive	Very direct
	Pursues change	Self-determined
	Confident	Organized
	Socially skilled	Traditional
	Inspiring	Goal-oriented
	Open	Dependable
	Direct	Economical
Affiliative	Outgoing	Ambitious
High		Low
	L	F
	Team-oriented	Exacting
	Caring	Thorough
	Devoted	Factual
	Enthusiastic	Reserved
	Helpful	Meticulous
	Accessible	Practical
	Trusting	Calm
	Sensitive *Directive*	Has high standards
	Good listener Low	Risk-avoider
	Good friend	
	Likes variety	
	Gregarious	
	Peacemaker	

LIMITATIONS

	S High	E
	Pushy	Dogmatic
	Intimidating	Stubborn
	Overbearing	Rigid
	Restless	Unapproachable
	Impatient	Distant
	Manipulative	Critical
	Abrasive	Insensitive
	Reactive	
Affiliative	Dominating	
High		Low
	L	F
	Too other-oriented	Slow to get things done
	Indecisive	Perfectionistic
	Impractical	Withdrawn
	Vulnerable	Dull
	Hesitant *Directive*	Sullen
	Subjective	Shy
	Low	Passive

APPENDIX A

SELF and Interactions with Others

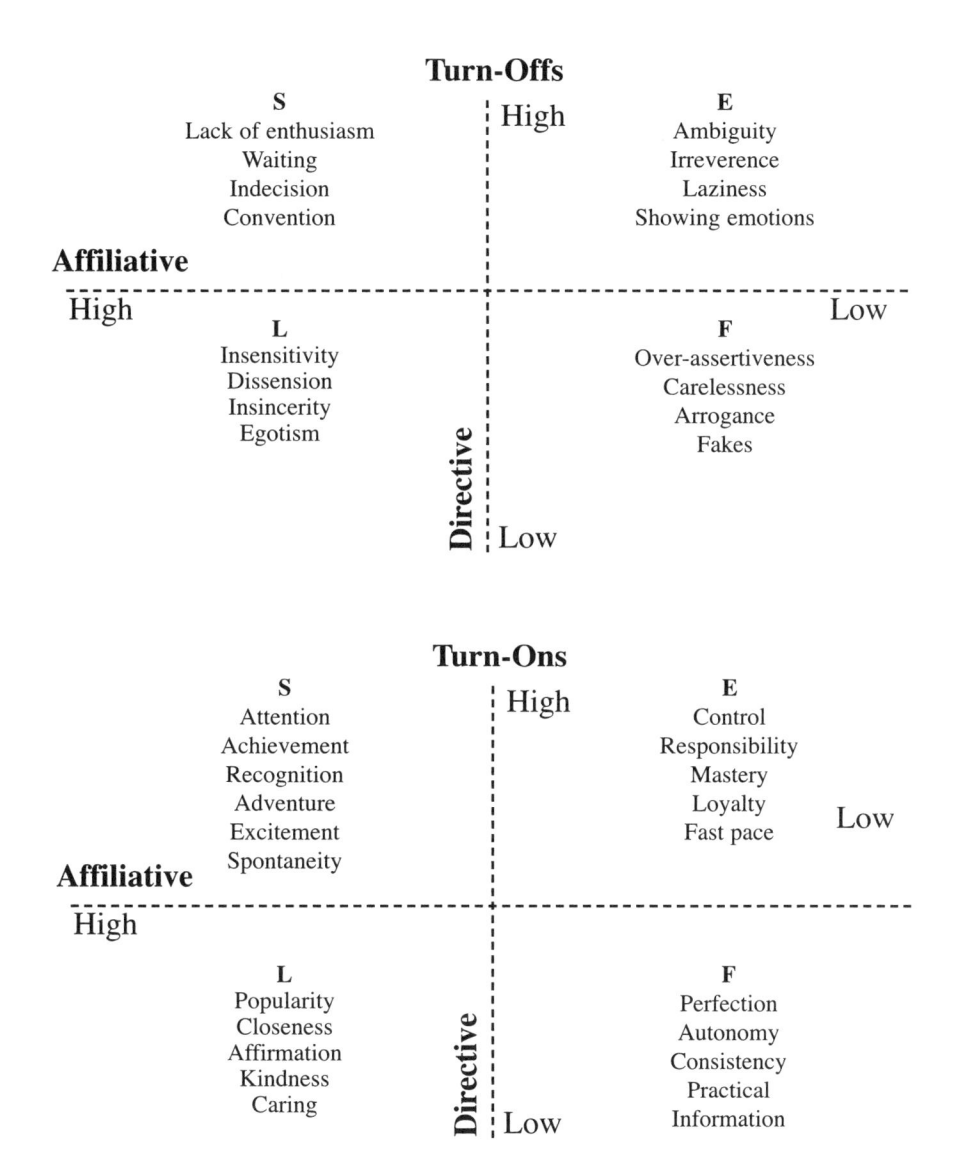

Turn-Offs

Affiliative High — **Low**

	High	
S Lack of enthusiasm Waiting Indecision Convention		**E** Ambiguity Irreverence Laziness Showing emotions
L Insensitivity Dissension Insincerity Egotism	**Directive**	**F** Over-assertiveness Carelessness Arrogance Fakes
	Low	

Turn-Ons

Affiliative High — **Low**

	High	
S Attention Achievement Recognition Adventure Excitement Spontaneity		**E** Control Responsibility Mastery Loyalty Fast pace
L Popularity Closeness Affirmation Kindness Caring	**Directive**	**F** Perfection Autonomy Consistency Practical Information
	Low	

101

How to Coach an Effective Team

Successful Working Strategies

If you are in a working relationship with someone of this style, here are a few things that may be helpful to remember.

If your supervisor/manager operates from one of these dimensions, it may be helpful to remember these guidelines.

For Working with Employees or Peers
DO

S
- Allow them the flexibility to be creative.
- They seek recognition and exciting challenges so reward their efforts with your enthusiasm.
- Channel their energy in appropriate directions (not always easy).
- Make sure they get lots of credit (they'll probably take it anyway).
- Respect need for socializing.
- Remember: We are important (philosophy).

E
- They need control — take advantage of their efficient, practical, ambitious nature and give them the reins when possible.
- Take advantage of their need to clear up messes — when business is bad or the situation ambiguous, they'll be the best people to provide structure and get others back on-line.
- Show respect for their traditional values and ways of thinking.
- Work with them to be more accepting of other methods of accomplishment.
- Remember: I am important (philosophy).

L
- Remember their need to keep everyone happy and their skill at keeping the peace — when business is good, these people will be the most effective leaders.
- Treat them fairly, supportively and openly.
- Allow them opportunities to interact with others.
- Appeal to their principles and values.
- Remember: They are important (philosophy).

F
- Listen, these people may not be the boldest or first to present ideas — be assured, however, that they have a lot of great ideas.
- Work with them to set deadlines (you may often have to help them see the virtues of "good enough").
- Give them space to operate.
- Pay attention and appreciate their need for substance and credibility.
- Recognize they are practical and emotional.
- Remember: It is important (philosophy).

For Working with Supervisors/Managers
DO

S
- Be sociable.
- Be flexible, open and spontaneous.
- Show enthusiasm and excitement.
- Let them get lots of credit.
- Provide support by providing balance between them and other employees, subtly interject reality when necessary and keep things tidy and organized.

E
- Recognize they are motivated by challenge.
- Play by their rules.
- Be on time, to the point, oriented toward results.
- Show that you are keenly aware of their authority.
- Provide support by serving as a buffer between them and other employees, expose them to alternative ways of doing things, but document everything with emphasis on results.

L
- Openly express your thoughts, concerns, ideas.
- Be a team player, compromise, strive for consensus, build relationships.
- Take interest in your supervisor/manager as a person.
- Make it easy for them when they have to be directive.
- Provide support; set your own performance goals and get them done.

F
- Acknowledge their expertise.
- Give facts and data, and be consistent.
- Think things through and document ideas with facts from credible sources.
- Offer detailed, well-thought-out plans of action.
- Provide support by subtly providing energy and enthusiasm through the ranks, bringing in fresh, new approaches (but be sure to document and detail every aspect of your proposal).

Appendix A

For Working with Employees or Peers **DON'T**	**For Working with Supervisors/Managers** **DON'T**

S

- Stifle their energy by demanding their conformity.
- Forget to show them your appreciation for their new and thoughtful ideas.
- Be too put off by their unconventionality; they are motivated by opportunities and friendship.

E

- Get into their "territory" (they'll let you know).
- "Go around" them on issues when they should be involved.
- Be ambiguous or use excuses.
- Exhibit unassertive behavior.

L

- Take advantage of their eagerness to please.
- Be harsh or insensitive.
- Forget to acknowledge them when you pass them in the hall.
- Criticize or cause conflicts.

F

- Pressure them, in the interest of expediency, to abandon their careful, exacting nature (it is these traits that keep the rest of us honest).
- Expect them to quickly get on board and initiate new projects without thinking them through first.
- Expect them to empathize (emotional) in a crisis; instead they'll use logic and practicality.

S

- Openly argue.
- Expect them to have everything organized and carefully laid out.
- Present one conclusion; instead explore possible compromise/ options.
- Use a win/loss approach.

E

- Exhibit any behaviors that may be misinterpreted as laziness (they'll look for it).
- Expect more than a "business relationship."
- Waste time chatting.
- Expect any strokes.

L

- Take advantage of their nature by slacking off.
- Forget the importance of maintaining social rapport and informal chats.
- Forget to listen and have patience.

F

- Be false and ingratiating — do your homework and stick to the facts.
- Be in a hurry to prove yourself or push through your new ideas.
- Appear arrogant or cocky.
- Expect a high risk or surprise in decision-making.

How to Coach an Effective Team

APPENDIX B

How to Coach an Effective Team

Thirteen Reasons People Don't Do What They're Supposed to Do …

	Appraise	Discipline	Terminate

1. They don't know they should do it.

2. They don't know how to do it.

3. They don't know what they are supposed to do.

4. They think your way will not work.

5. They think their way is better.

6. They think something else is more important

7. There is no positive outcome to them for doing it.

8. They think they are doing it.

9. They are rewarded for not doing it.

10. They are punished for doing it.

11. They anticipate negative consequences.

12. No negative consequence exists for poor attempts.

13. Obstacles exist that exceed their control.

Adapted from *Why Employees Don't Do What They're Supposed to Do and What to Do About It*. Ferdinand Fournies, Liberty House Press, 1988.

INDEX

A
Appreciation   7, 36, 44

B
Barriers
    Independent spirit   5
    Spirit of competition   5
Build relationships   15
Building confidence   54
Building involvement   30
Burger Technique   17-18, 73

C
Characteristics of an effective leader   3, 22, 29
Clarifying performance expectations   43
Coach Joe Says   6-8, 26, 38, 41, 46-47, 58, 61-64, 66, 75, 78
Coaching skills
    Ability to motivate   9
    Value team members   9
    Create a vision   10
    Inspire team members   10
Comfort zones   4, 6, 85-86
Communication skills   6, 24, 44, 55, 85
Confidentiality   45

Conflict resolution   8
Confrontation   4, 66, 71-73
Constructive criticism   24-25
Counseling   2-4, 11, 13, 29, 33, 62, 69-80, 86
Creativity   10, 38, 40, 54, 88

D
Delegating   29, 70
Diversity   3, 44-45, 77

E
Effective listening   15
Effective team   1, 3-5, 7, 9-11, 13, 29, 38, 43, 55
Empowerment   2, 22
Enthusiasm   2, 23, 26, 35, 38, 88
Evaluation   21, 25, 38
Exchange of ideas   21

F
Feedback   19, 21, 29, 36, 40, 53, 73, 76-77, 81, 86
Five-Step Staff Coaching Model   31, 33
Flexibility   23, 25, 34

H
Hands-on coach   46-47
Humor and spontaneity   37

I
Informal climate   1, 3
Integrity   22, 39, 89

INDEX

L
Lasorda, Tommy   54
Leading   3-4, 8, 10, 26, 30, 37-39, 90
Listening skills   3, 6, 24, 75, 80
Lombardi, Vince   44
Low self-esteem   24, 61

M
Mentoring   4, 11, 29, 33, 57-67, 86, 88
Motivating
    Money   16, 46
    Praise   7, 16-19, 29, 46
    Recognition   7, 16, 19-20, 35, 46, 51, 87-89
    Special awards   20
Motivational influence   7

N
Negative vs. positive words   25, 53, 55
Networking   29, 59
Non-verbal communication   53
Nurturing   7

O
Open-ended questions   54, 74, 86
Optimism   23, 35

P
Parker, Glenn   3
Peer training   70
People skills   2, 6, 8-9, 11, 69, 83, 85-86
Performance misconceptions   3-4
Peters, Tom   iii, 10, 30
Pitfalls   4, 50-52, 65
Proactive approach   36
Problem solving   2, 6, 8, 15, 35, 40, 44, 76, 85
Provide opportunity for training   14

R

Reasons some leaders don't coach   4, 48
Recognition   7, 16, 19-20, 35, 46, 51, 87-89
Reflections   12, 18, 27, 42, 56, 67, 81, 90-91
Respect   4, 24, 30, 71, 89
Response styles   20, 24
Robinson, Jackie   58

S

SELF Profile   24, 44
Seven deadly sins   24
Shared leadership   3
Six-step action plan   21
SMART goals   86-87
Smart questions   64, 66
Speaking skills   29
Successful leaders   1, 3, 8-9, 13, 20-23, 25, 29-31, 38, 45, 47, 49, 60, 85, 87

T

Teachable spirit   58-59, 62
Team goals   1-4, 6-7, 10, 20-21, 23, 29-30, 32, 34, 41, 44-45, 47-48, 51-52, 69, 76, 78, 87
Team stages
    Structuring stage   1, 8
    Settling stage   2
    Problem-solving stage   2
    Learning stage   2
    Performing stage   2
Team-building activities   6
Tone of trust   4
Trust   1-2, 4, 6, 19, 22, 30, 37, 45, 61, 74-75, 88-89

W

Wooden, John   73

Buy any 3, get 1 FREE!

Get a 60-Minute Training Series™ Handbook FREE ($14.95 value)* when you buy any three. See back of order form for full selection of titles.

These are helpful how-to books for you, your employees and co-workers. Add to your library. Use for new-employee training, brown-bag seminars, promotion gifts and more. Choose from many popular titles on a variety of lifestyle, communication, productivity and leadership topics exclusively from National Press Publications.

BUY 3 GET 1 FREE! Buy more, save more!

DESKTOP HANDBOOK ORDER FORM

Ordering is easy:

1. Complete both sides of this Order Form, detach, and mail, fax or phone your order to:

   Mail: National Press Publications
   P.O. Box 419107
   Kansas City, MO 64141-6107

   Fax: 1-913-432-0824
   Phone: 1-800-258-7248
   Internet: www.NationalSeminarsTraining.com

2. Please print:

   Name_____ Position/Title _____
   Company/Organization_____
   Address_____City _____
   State/Province_____ZIP/Postal Code _____
   Telephone (____)_____ Fax (____)_____
   Your e-mail: _____

3. Easy payment:
   ❏ Enclosed is my check or money order for $_____ (total from back).
   Please make payable to National Press Publications.

   Please charge to:
   ❏ MasterCard ❏ VISA ❏ American Express
   Credit Card No. _____ Exp. Date _____
   Signature_____

   •
   MORE WAYS TO SAVE:
   SAVE 33%!!! BUY 20-50 COPIES of any title ... pay just $9.95 each ($13.25 Canadian).
   SAVE 40%!!! BUY 51 COPIES OR MORE of any title ... pay just $8.95 each ($11.95 Canadian).
   *$20.00 in Canada

VIP No. 922 008438 099

Buy 3, get 1 FREE!
60-MINUTE TRAINING SERIES™ HANDBOOKS

TITLE	ITEM #	RETAIL PRICE*	QTY	TOTAL
8 Steps for Highly Effective Negotiations	#424	$14.95		
Assertiveness	#4422	$14.95		
Balancing Career and Family	#4152	$14.95		
Common Ground	#4122	$14.95		
Delegate for Results	#4592	$14.95		
The Essentials of Business Writing	#4310	$14.95		
Everyday Parenting Solutions	#4862	$14.95		
Exceptional Customer Service	#4882	$14.95		
Fear & Anger: Slay the Dragons …	#4302	$14.95		
Fundamentals of Planning	#4301	$14.95		
Getting Things Done	#4112	$14.95		
How to Coach an Effective Team	#4308	$14.95		
How to De-Junk Your Life	#4306	$14.95		
How to Handle Conflict and Confrontation	#4952	$14.95		
How to Manage Your Boss	#493	$14.95		
How to Supervise People	#4102	$14.95		
How to Work With People	#4032	$14.95		
Inspire & Motivate: Performance Reviews	#4232	$14.95		
Listen Up: Hear What's Really Being Said	#4172	$14.95		
Motivation and Goal-Setting	#4962	$14.95		
A New Attitude	#4432	$14.95		
The New Dynamic Comm. Skills for Women	#4309	$14.95		
The Polished Professional	#4262	$14.95		
The Power of Innovative Thinking	#428	$14.95		
The Power of Self-Managed Teams	#4222	$14.95		
Powerful Communication Skills	#4132	$14.95		
Present With Confidence	#4612	$14.95		
The Secret to Developing Peak Performers	#4692	$14.95		
Self-Esteem: The Power to Be Your Best	#4642	$14.95		
Shortcuts to Organized Files & Records	#4307	$14.95		
The Stress Management Handbook	#4842	$14.95		
Supreme Teams: How to Make Teams Work	#4303	$14.95		
Thriving on Change	#4212	$14.95		
Women and Leadership	#4632	$14.95		

Sales Tax
All purchases subject to state and local sales tax.
Questions?
Call
1-800-258-7248

Subtotal		$
Add 7% Sales Tax *(Or add appropriate state and local tax)*		$
Shipping and Handling** *($6 one item; 50¢ each additional item)*		$
TOTAL		$

**Free Freight on all orders over $150.00   *$20.00 in Canada